Home Office Research Study 249

The economic and social costs of Class A drug use in England and Wales, 2000

Christine Godfrey, Gail Eaton, Cynthia McDougall and Anthony Culyer

The views expressed in this report are those of the authors, not necessarily those of the Home Office (nor do they reflect Government policy).

Home Office Research, Development and Statistics Directorate
November 2002

Home Office Research Studies

The Home Office Research Studies are reports on research undertaken by or on behalf of the Home Office. They cover the range of subjects for which the Home Secretary has responsibility. Other publications produced by the Research, Development and Statistics Directorate include Findings, Statistical Bulletins and Statistical Papers.

The Research, Development and Statistics Directorate

RDS is part of the Home Office. The Home Office's purpose is to build a safe, just and tolerant society in which the rights and responsibilities of individuals, families and communities are properly balanced and the protection and security of the public are maintained.

RDS is also part of National Statistics (NS). One of the aims of NS is to inform Parliament and the citizen about the state of the nation and provide a window on the work and performance of government, allowing the impact of government policies and actions to be assessed.

Therefore –

Research Development and Statistics Directorate exists to improve policy making, decision taking and practice in support of the Home Office purpose and aims, to provide the public and Parliament with information necessary for informed debate and to publish information for future use.

First published 2002

Application for reproduction should be made to the Communication Development Unit, Room 201, Home Office, 50 Queen Anne's Gate, London SW1H 9AT.

© Crown copyright 2002   ISBN 1 84082 874 9

ISSN 0072 6435

Foreword

Estimates of the economic and social costs of Class A drug use in England and Wales are an important addition to the growing evidence base supporting the Government's anti-drugs strategy. This information is valuable both for policy makers and for directing future research into what works in reducing illicit drug consumption, not least in terms of crime reduction and value for money.

The main findings from the study provide the first real evidence that costs are mostly associated with problematic drug use and drug-related crime, in particular acquisitive crime. In addition, significant cost consequences are identified for health care services, the criminal justice system and state benefits.

As with any modelling exercise, the cost estimates reported in this study are far from perfect, but the key assumptions used and gaps in evidence have been made explicit. Overall, an important step has been made and the model developed in this report provides a good foundation for estimating future economic and social costs of Class A drug misuse when new data become available, and to track the economic impact of the Government's proactive expenditure on anti-drugs policies.

DAVID PYLE
Drugs and Alcohol Research Unit
Research, Development and Statistics Directorate

Acknowledgements

We are extremely grateful to the Home Office for funding this research and to them and the Office of National Statistics for providing data from the British Crime Survey and the Youth Lifestyle Survey. The research was guided by a team drawn from a number of departments and this team provided valuable feedback and comment. We also expressed considerable thanks to the National Treatment Outcome Research Study team at the National Addiction Centre, funded by the Department of Health, particularly Duncan Stewart and Michael Gossop, for their help and additional analysis of their data conducted at our request. Steve Parrott also provided considerable support to the project. Finally, two anonymous referees provided very useful comments on an earlier draft of the report.

The Authors

Christine Godfrey, Professor of Health Economics, Department of Health Sciences and Centre for Health Economics, University of York.

Gail Eaton, Research Fellow, Centre for Criminal Justice, Economics and Psychology, University of York.

Cynthia McDougall, Professor of Psychology, Centre for Criminal Justice, Economics and Psychology, University of York.

Anthony Culyer, Professor of Economics, Department of Economics and Related Studies, University of York.

Contents

Summary

Introduction: developing the methodology (Chapter 1)

This research study provides estimates of the economic and social costs of Class A drug use in England and Wales for the year 2000. The methodology used to estimate costs will also enable future simulations of the relationship between various streams of government proactive and reactive expenditure.

Figure 1.1 provides an overview of the costing methodology. Class A drug users are first identified by type of user: young recreational, older regular, and problematic. Prevalence estimates are derived for each type of drug user using established methods reported in the literature. Consequences by type of drug user are derived from available treatment data. Unit costs are then applied to the consequences where reliable data are available – mainly health care services, the criminal justice system, and state benefits.

Total economic costs, defined as government reactive expenditure, are estimated by adding all the various cost consequences identified for each drug user type. Adding victim costs of crime and value for premature deaths to other resource costs results in total economic and social costs. Other potential social costs are indentified but not included in the final estimates.

An important aspect of the costing methodology is the separation of consequences and costs according to whether or not problem drug users are receiving treatment. Chapter 3 demonstrates that problem drug users account for the majority of total economic and social costs. Consequences and costs are also provided for young recreational and older regular drug users, but in comparison to the costs of problem drug use, these estimates are small.

Further developments of the model are considered in terms of the definition of user groups and consequences (Figure 1.3 and Table 1.1). The proposed typology of consequences comprises five domains (health, work, driving, crime and other social impacts) and six different groups who may bear the costs (users, families/carers, other individuals directly affected, wider community effects, industry, and the public sector).

Estimating the number of drug users (Chapter 2)

Estimates of the total number of users of Class A drugs are presented as well as numbers in different groups. The estimates relate to the year 2000 for England and Wales, and are derived by updating previous estimates reported in the literature.

There is uncertainty with all methods for estimating the number of Class A drug users, but in particular for problematic drug users. Given this uncertainty, three methods are considered to derive a range of estimates for problem drug users: the multivariate indicator method, the treatment coverage method, and the treatment demographic method. The last method produces the lowest estimate of 281,125 (see below), but is closer to previously reported estimates in the literature.

Prevalence estimates for all types of Class A drug user are:

Number of young recreational users of Class A drugs:
399,000 (lowest estimate)
798,000 (highest estimate)

Number of older regular users of Class A drugs:
1,091,000 (lowest estimate)
2,182.000 (highest estimate)

Class A problem users in England and Wales:
281,125 (lowest estimate)
337,350 (medium estimate)
506,025(highest estimate)

The total number of Class A drug users is the sum of problem drug users, young recreational users and older regular users. The low and high estimates to the nearest thousand are calculated from the sums of appropriate figures. The medium estimate is calculated from summing the low estimate of the young recreational and older regular users with the medium estimate of problem drug users. This yields the following range of estimates:

Total number of Class A drug users:
1,771,000 (low)
1,827,000 (medium)
3,486,000 (high)

Estimating the cost consequences (Chapter 3)

Data with which to estimate the economic and social costs of drug misuse are notoriously scarce. However, significant information was available for problem drug users who account for the majority of total costs. Most data for consequences come from the National Treatment Outcomes Research Study (NTORS) and comprise health care services, the criminal justice system, and employment.

Cost consequences are identified for each type of drug user: recreational, older regular and problematic. For the last group, consequences are identified according to whether or not they are in treatment, and then by duration of treatment (less than or more than one year).

Consequences identified include health care services: GP, Accident and Emergency, hospital days, mental health services; state benefits; and criminal justice system: police arrests/acquisitive crime, police custody, court appearances, and prison. In addition, a number of other health care costs are identified, such as those associated with injecting, but not included in the final estimates.

A total of £6 million a year health service and criminal justice costs was associated with young recreational users. This translates to a cost of £7.50 to £15 per user depending on whether the lower or higher estimate of the number of young recreational users is used. Total social costs for this group was estimated at £28.8 million a year, a cost per user between £36 and £72. These social costs include an estimate of the full costs of premature deaths from ecstasy use. Older regular users were estimated to cost around £6.2 million each year, a cost per user between £3 and £6. Estimates for young recreational and older regular users exclude any allowance for productivity effects and effects from driving and drug taking.

For problem drug users, total economic costs range from £2.9bn to £5.3bn, based on low to high estimates of the number of problem drug users (the medium estimate is £3.5bn) – £10,402 per user per annum. Total economic and social costs for this group increase the range of figures to between £10.1bn and £17.4bn – £35,455 per user per annum.

Problem drug users account for almost all economic and social costs (99%), and drug-related crime accounts for around 88 per cent of total economic and social costs.

Summary and conclusions (Chapter 4)

The economic and social costs of Class A drug misuse provided in this research report represents the first real attempt at assigning monetary values to a difficult problem to society. Estimates are based on the most reliable data available and an innovative model that examines major cost consequences according to the treatment status of problem drug users. The design of the costing model will allow future updates on economic and social costs, as well as future simulations of the relationship between streams of government proactive and reactive expenditure.

As with any modelling exercise there are bound to be a number of assumptions and limitations that need to be considered when interpreting results. These will need to be updated when new data become available. These have been made explicit in each chapter of the report (as well as recommendations for future research), but a few key assumptions are discussed in more detail. Sensitivity analyses of key assumptions suggest that the range of estimates provided for the economic and social costs of Class A drug misuse are fairly robust.

1. Introduction: developing the methodology

Aims of the project

In a previous project, the methodology and evidence to consider the costing of substance misuse were reviewed (Culyer *et al.*, 2002). A costing methodology was required to estimate reactive government expenditure on substance misuse. This research study provides estimates of these economic costs and the wider social costs of Class A drug use in England and Wales for the year 2000.

The methodology also needed to be robust to allow future simulations of the relationship between various streams of government proactive and reactive expenditures. Proactive government expenditure is defined as that spending which has the clearly stated objective of reducing drug use or problems. Reactive government expenditure is expenditure incurred which does not directly reduce either the prevalence of drug use or drug-related consequences but is the result of some consequence related to drug use. Estimating the flows of public expenditure is a necessary component of the regular Comprehensive Spending Reviews (CSR). The full economic and social costs are based on the impact of drug use on resource costs in the economy.

Developing the methodology

The proposed costing model is a general one that could be adapted for all substances, legal and illegal. In Figure 1.1 the links between users and consequences are expanded to indicate how economic estimates could be derived. The first step illustrated by the first box in the diagram involves estimation of the prevalence of total drug users and the numbers in the different groups identified in the typology. The next step involves estimating the prevalence of different consequences that can be attributed to the drug users of different types. This stage of the process will be dependent on the research available to identify these consequences. Prevalence estimates can then be combined with estimates of the unit costs of each type of consequence to yield the economic and social cost estimates. This process would need to distinguish between resource and public expenditure flows.

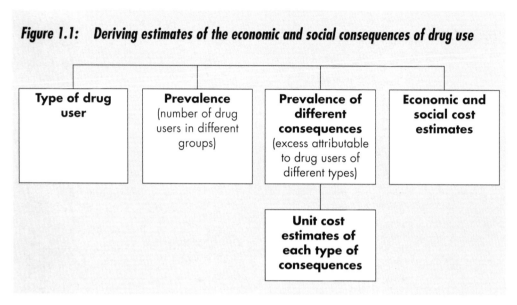

Figure 1.1:   Deriving estimates of the economic and social consequences of drug use

Defining the user groups

In the previous project a typology of illicit drug users was proposed. Three mutually exclusive groups were proposed, see Figure 1.2. These groups were:

- young recreational users – defined as those taking Class A drugs aged under 25 but not in the problem user group;
- older regular users – defined as those regularly taking Class A drugs aged 25 or over but not in the problem user group; and
- problem users – users of any age whose drug use is no longer controlled or undertaken for recreational purposes and where drugs have become a more essential element of the individual's life.

In theory these groups are defined not by the type of drugs consumed but by the intensity of use and problems related to that intensity. That is, if drugs are an essential component of the individual's life and the individual is experiencing problems related to that intensity of use; the individual would be defined as a problem user. If the user does not consume at that level or with problems then those aged under 25 would be in the young recreational user group and those aged 25 and over would be in the older regular user group. This does not mean that younger recreational users or older regular user would not be associated with any harmful consequences but such problems are rarer and/or associated with using drugs in specific circumstances, for example, while driving.

Figure 1.2: *Expanding the type of drug users*

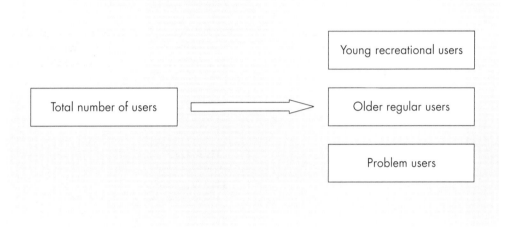

The total number of users is the sum of the numbers in each of these three groups. Different consequences are linked with these three groups. There are two additional sub-types of drug users. Within the young recreational users group there is a sub-group of particular policy interest. These are the young people with a number of characteristics or in social circumstances which put them at high risk of moving from recreational to problem use. Reducing the number in the high-risk group would result in lower numbers being in the problem use group in future time periods.

The second sub-group is within the problem user group. Injecting drug use is associated with a number of additional health problems. Infectious disease risks in particular could have large consequences for the user, and additional demand for health services and risk of disease in the wider community. It was thought important therefore to define injecting users as a sub-group of problem users. In developing the methodology and attempting to provide empirical estimates, however, further divisions amongst this group seemed desirable. Some risks, for example, infected injecting sites' are related to current injecting status. Other consequences depend on the disease state of the drug user. Past drug injectors may be infected with a different disease but do not know their current disease status. Current drug injectors with disease-free status continue to be at risk. It did prove possible to estimate numbers of current and past injectors but not to provide separate estimates of the consequences of past and current injectors.

Refining the types of consequences

To start estimating costs, decisions need to be taken on the type of consequences that will be included or excluded. Economists in any study can take either a positive or normative viewpoint. The normative viewpoint involves value judgements about what "ought to be". For example, one viewpoint could be that drug users make a choice as to whether to take or not to take drugs. If users are economically rational in this sense it could be assumed that they take potential individual costs and benefits of the drug use into account when making their decisions. This would imply, in the normative framework, that governments should not concern themselves with private individual costs of drug use but only be concerned about those consequences that impact on the rest of society. There has been work on different normative frameworks and their relevance to drugs of addiction and dependence covering concepts such as rational addiction (see for example Buck *et al.*, 1996). Models have been proposed about the range of costs of drug use and the benefits of drug consumption, both of legal and illegal substances, from the user's perspective which should be considered in a policy-making framework under different assumptions. These assumptions include the level of information and the nature of addiction or dependence. The models can be further extended to explore the impact of different types of policies on the patterns of costs and consequences of drug use. For example, tax policies on legal drugs or drug possession enforcement policies can be seen as coercive by reducing the benefits of consumption of those who have not created costs for other members of society. This contrasts to education programmes or voluntary treatments which would not be associated with the same forced behaviour change and loss of consumption benefits (Godfrey and Maynard, 1995). Within the current proposed methodology the pattern of costs and benefits under such normative frameworks would be expected to vary across the different drug user types. Older regular users are by definition assumed to be taking economically rational decisions and do not have a dependent pattern of use.

A positive viewpoint by economists starts from the premise that economists can enumerate all costs and consequences from a neutral standpoint and present these data to the decision-maker in order that they can make a decision based on their values (or democratically reflected values). In costing frameworks, however, it is difficult to maintain an entirely "normative" free framework as all items identified have to be assigned a value and this process of assigning values to concepts such as the loss of life will involve some value judgements. A positive viewpoint was adopted in this project to allow maximum flexibility in the methodology.

The costing estimates presented here represent the baseline against which the effects of any changes in policy could be assessed. The figures in this report estimate the economic and social costs, given current policies and other circumstances. Using the methods described in this report, different estimates can then be made under alternative policy assumptions.

Following the positive economic framework, it seems sensible to develop the typology of consequences according to who bears the cost. Six separate groups are identified in Figure 1.3:

- users;
- families/carers;
- other individuals directly affected;
- wider community effects;
- industry; and
- public sector.

Figure 1.3: *Expanding the types of consequences*

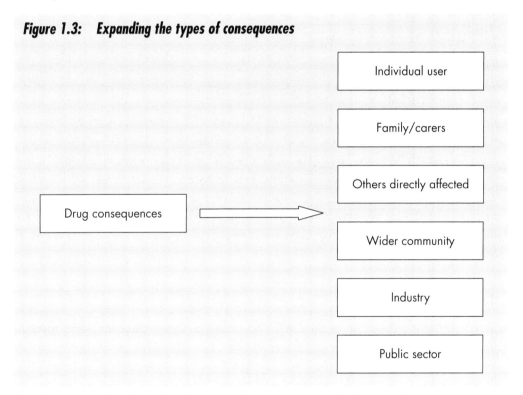

The domains of the effects: health; work; driving; crime and other social consequences can then be considered for each group. The total sum of costs across sectors or across all parties would need adjusting so that there was no double counting of the same consequence. There is also a need, following the logic of the costing model, to map consequences to the different types of drug users as was outlined in Culyer *et al.*, 2002. Another extension of the model would be to consider the "economic" benefits of drug use especially as experienced by the individual. Such benefits as suggested may be affected by different policies. This was, however, outside the scope of the current project.

Each of the different groups now requires further work to identify all the potential consequences of Class A drugs. Table 1.1 is an attempt to identify consequences for each of the six different groups who may bear the costs of drug use.

Table 1.1: *Examples of the typology of costs*

Group – Bearer of Cost	Examples of cost
Users	Premature death Loss of quality of life – mental and physical health; relationships; etc. Impact on educational achievement, training opportunities etc. Excess unemployment and loss of lifetime earnings
Families/carers	Impact on children of drug users Transmission of infections Intergeneration impact on drug use Financial problems Concern/worry for users Caring for drug users or drug users' dependants
Other individuals directly affected	Victims of drug driving; drug-related violence; drug-related crime Transmission of infections from drug users
Wider community effects	Fear of crime Environmental aspects of drug markets – needles, effects of drug dealing in community etc.
Industry	Sickness absence Theft in the workplace Security expenditure to prevent drug-related crime Productivity losses Impact of illicit markets on legitimate markets
Public sector	Health care expenditure Criminal justice expenditure Social care services Social security benefits

The consequences outlined in Table 1.1 would need to be identified, measured and valued. There are concerns about how to measure and value different consequences. Productivity losses frequently account for a large proportion of estimated social costs of drugs, but it is unclear how to estimate and value lower productivity associated with health or drug problems. In the short-term, the loss of productivity may be partially compensated by other workers and in the longer-term the labour market may adjust to these impacts especially from general recreational use. Also some consequences are difficult to value in monetary terms, for example, what value can be put on the loss of life or the fear of crime. Table 1.1 provides a checklist against which available empirical estimates can be compared. In practice it proved difficult to find any empirical data to measure and value a number of items, particularly those borne by families and carers.

As shown in Figure 1.4 some of the consequences can be further sub-divided. In particular it is important for the public sector to distinguish resource consequences from transfers. Transfers refer to public finance expenditures, e.g., social security benefits, which do not in themselves affect the total resources in the economy but signal a movement of resources from one section of the population (tax payers) to another (benefit-claiming drug users).

Figure 1.4: Expanding the types of public sector consequences

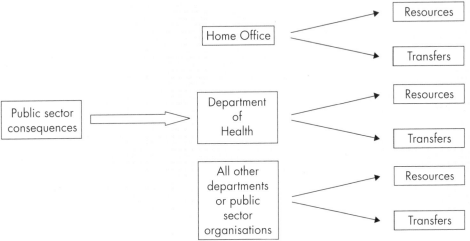

For illicit drugs there is clearly a lack of information at many points, from prevalence of drug use, consequences and the effectiveness and costs of policies. The current model is therefore proposed not as a part of any exact decision-making model but rather as an exploratory tool.

The estimation of the number of users in the different groups is given in Chapter 2 with cost consequences detailed in Chapter 3. Chapters 2 and 3 contain a summary of the assumptions made, i.e. an assumptions log. Comments are also provided on further research and gaps in data currently available for Chapters 1-3. Chapter 4 provides a summary of the results and a discussion of the limitations of the research.

Further research

- All the current work depends on the rapid review undertaken for Culyer *et al.*, (2002). There is potential to expand and improve on the model with more specific reviews and adopting other modelling methodology techniques (Godfrey *et al.*, 2001).

- The normative framework of costing studies and, in particular, the techniques required to obtain an estimate of the benefits of drug use under different assumptions, would provide a fuller range of estimates for the policy-makers to consider.

2.   Estimating the number of drug users

Introduction

This chapter provides estimates of numbers of users of Class A drugs: cocaine, crack, ecstasy, heroin, methadone, LSD and magic mushrooms. It is not concerned with dipipanone, morphine, opium, pethidine, phenylcyclidine, cannabinol and cannabinol derivatives nor does it directly consider Class B drugs prepared for injecting, except amphetamine. Sources for all estimates are discussed within the chapter. A full assumption log is provided and suggestions made for future research and data gathering which may improve these estimates. Prevalence estimates are provided for England and Wales for the year 2000.

The total number of drug users is the sum of young recreational users, older regular users and problem drug users. If an estimate of the total number of users is available and problem use can be defined, the other groups would be defined by default.

Problem drug use would ideally be defined in relationship to an individual's experiences. There is no agreed definition of a problem user (see review in Culyer *et al.*, 2002). Problem drug users are generally understood to be those whose drug use is no longer controlled or undertaken for recreational purposes and where drugs have become a more essential element of an individual's life. Estimates are generally based on the numbers in treatment or with other identified major drug-related problems. Problem use can be assumed as starting some time before people report for treatment, or some estimate is made of the proportion of the problem drug using population actually receiving treatment at any one point of time. It proved, however, more difficult to define non-problem users without making some assumptions based on the drugs used.

Problem drug use is associated with certain drugs, opiates and cocaine, as well as injecting drug use of amphetamines. However, not all consumers of these drugs are currently problem users. The estimates of problem drug users were higher than the estimate of all users of these drugs based on population surveys. Therefore, to estimate the number of young recreational and older regular users, some division had to be made from these surveys of problematic and non-problematic use. It was assumed therefore that all opiate use and crack use reported in such surveys is problematic; this assumption may be revised in time if better evidence and monitoring data become available. All ecstasy, LSD and magic mushroom use is assumed not to be problematic. Cocaine use, on the basis of evidence from the BCS for 2000 (Ramsey et al., 2001), can be assumed to be both recreational and problematic. These issues and more detailed estimates are provided in the following text.

Problem drug users

A number of reports base estimates of prevalence of problem drug use on modelling techniques identified by EMCDDA (1997) and tested by Frischer et al. (2001) for the UK. Estimates are for different types of problems; problem drug users, problem opiate users, opiate users at risk of death and injecting drug users; each estimated through using one or more models.

Estimates provided by Frischer et al. are for 1996 and, while considered plausible by the authors, limitations of methods are noted. In the previous project (Culyer et al., 2002), it was suggested prevalence be based, where possible, on these modelling techniques to provide more up-to-date estimates of use of Class A drugs for England and Wales.

The *Multivariate Indicator Method* combines information on prevalence that is available in only a few localities and 'indicators' or 'predictors' of drug use that are available in all areas: convictions for drug offences; seizures of controlled drugs; treatment populations; numbers of drug-related HIV and drug-related deaths. A key assumption is that the relationship between prevalence in a few localities and the predictors is transferable to all locations. From this method, the 1996 estimate for problem drug users in the UK was 268,000. There are a number of limitations for replication of this method, not least the lack of time-relevant prevalence data. We therefore do not attempt to use this method to estimate prevalence of problem use of Class A drugs in England and Wales.

The *Treatment Demographic Method,* used to estimate the number of problem opiate users, involves calculating the product of the number of users entering treatment in any year for the first time and the average life duration of problem opiate use prior to entering treatment. The total number of incident cases was estimated from the Regional Drug Misuse Database (RDMD). Mean duration was estimated to be eight years by Frischer et al., 2001. For the UK, in 1996, 162,544 problem opiate users were estimated.

This method for estimating the number of problem users of Class A drugs has been replicated using data on those reporting for treatment from October 1999 to September 2000, the latest available data (Department of Health, 2001a). Extrapolation from the

Regional Drug Misuse Databases (RDMD) requires two six- monthly reporting periods being added together and therefore there may be double counting of individuals reporting twice within a twelve month period, although this is assumed to be small. Frischer *et al.* (2001) used an estimate of eight years before a user would enter treatment. This could be thought excessive, especially given the recent expansion of available treatment. A more realistic time-scale for duration of problem use to entry into treatment has been taken to be five years, based on Coid *et al.* (2000). However, this assumption is based on only one study. Shortening the time period in this way acts to reduce the estimate of problem drug users.

For England and Wales RDMD data suggest 55,043 problem opiate and cocaine users new to treatment. There were, in addition, 2,955 users reporting amphetamines as main drug, between 38 per cent and 41per cent, (of these an average of 40%), 1,182, report injecting (and are therefore classed as Class A users). 56,225 users of Class A drugs newly reporting, multiplied by five years is equal to 281,125 problem Class A users. This is a much higher estimate than reported for 1996 for the UK for opiate users.

Treatment Demographic Method:
Number of Class A problem users in England and Wales is 281,125

A second method of estimating the number of problem opiate users tested by Frischer *et al.* is the *Treatment Coverage Method*. This method extrapolates from the number of opiate users in treatment in a given year and assumes a 25 per cent coverage. These assumptions (as with the previous method) are not based on strong evidence, but often on expert opinion or limited observational studies. To use this method requires extrapolating from the RDMD, which currently reports only on new episodes; Frischer *et al.* assume this to represent a third of those in treatment. Based on this method they estimate 243,820 problem opiate users in the UK.

Using this method to estimate problem use of Class A drugs in England and Wales, it is also assumed new episodes represent a third of those in treatment. This assumption will soon be able to be tested via the new treatment monitoring system, the National Drugs Treatment Monitoring System (NDTMS), which will be prevalence-based, rather than incidence-based. It is also assumed, given an increase in treatment following new funding, there will be a greater coverage and it is assumed to be between 33 per cent and 50 per cent currently in treatment rather than 25 per cent assumed by Frischer *et al.* With 56,225 users of Class A drugs new to treatment from October 1999 to September 2000 we assume 168,675 in treatment. Assuming a 50 per cent coverage we estimate approximately 337,350 problem

Class A users in England and Wales. Assuming a 33 per cent coverage we estimate approximately 506,025 problem Class A users in England and Wales.

Treatment Coverage Method:
Number of Class A problem users in England and Wales between 337,350 and 506,025

Both of these estimates of problem users may require revision on the basis of improved monitoring now being established, and further research evidence.

Applying these methods yields three estimates and it is suggested that these are used as high, low and medium estimates.

Number of Class A problem users in England and Wales:
281,125 (lowest estimate)
337,350 (medium estimate)
506,025(highest estimate)

Injecting users

Frischer *et al.* applied the *HIV Multiplier Method* to estimate the number of injecting drug users. Estimates of the number of injectors with HIV infection are multiplied by estimates of the proportion of the injecting population infected with HIV. From this method they estimate 161, 200 injecting users in the UK.

This method relates only to lifetime injecting drug users and assumes that all alive HIV positive injectors are still current injectors and also that the prevalence of HIV and the number infected move in unison. Both estimates are assumed by Frischer *et al.* (2001) to be suspect.

They also provided an estimate based on the BCS and Anderson and Frischer (1997), suggesting 168,905 injecting users in the UK. Both estimates are similar and the mean is 165,000.

It is not possible to use these methods, given the problem with the first method and the fact that the BCS no longer asks respondents about injecting. However, from models used by Frischer *et al.*, injecting drug users represent 80 per cent (165,000 injecting users as a percentage of 203,000 problem opiate users) of all problem opiate users (this will not include injectors of cocaine-based drugs and amphetamines).

If it is assumed that 80 per cent of problem Class A users inject, it can be estimated that there are 224,900 injecting users (based on the *Treatment Demographic Method* estimate of 281,125 problem Class A users) and between 269,880 and 404,820 (based on the *Treatment Coverage Method* estimate of between 337,350 and 506,025 problem Class A users).

Number of Class A injecting drug users in England and Wales:
224,900 (lowest estimate) (80% of 281,125)
269,880 (medium estimate) (80% of 337,350
404,820 (highest estimate) (80% of 506,025)

To estimate consequences, estimates of both current and past injectors could be useful. Current injectors are at higher risk of physical health problems associated with injecting, and at higher risk of overdose and death. Those current injectors not already infected with HIV, and/or hepatitis B, and/or hepatitis C also risk infection. Those already infected must be estimated separately. Former injectors will not currently be at risk of physical health problems associated with injecting, and at less risk of overdose and death. However, some may be infected already and these need to be estimated. Other former injectors will not have acquired infection but are at risk of relapse into injecting.

One means of estimating current and past injecting is to base assumptions on the proportion of injecting users in treatment, both current and ever injectors. From October 1999 to September 2000, of those whose injecting status was reported, 59 per cent were known current injectors and 41 per cent past injectors.

Using the *Treatment Demographic Method* estimate of 224,900 problem Class A injecting users, would suggest 132,691 current injectors, and based on the *Treatment Coverage Method* estimate of between 269,880 and 404,820 of injecting problem Class A users, between 199,036 and 238,844 current injectors.

Number of current injectors of Class A drugs in England and Wales:
132,691 (lowest estimate) (59% of 224,900)
159,229 (medium estimate) (59% of 269,880)
238,844 (highest estimate) (59% of 404,820)

Similarly, using the *Treatment Demographic Method* this would yield an estimate of 92,209 past injectors, and based on the *Treatment Coverage Method* between 110,651 and 165,976 past injectors.

Number of past injectors of Class A drugs in England and Wales:
92,209 (lowest estimate) (41% of 224,900)
110,651 (medium estimate) (41% of 269,880)
165,976 (highest estimate) (41% of 404,820)

Young recreational users

It could be expected that household and school surveys may provide the estimate of total drug users and therefore younger recreational users and older regular users would be defined as the residual after having excluded problem users. However, surveys yield estimates of users of Class A drugs such as opiates below those estimated above from treatment data. Without better data, therefore, all use of ecstasy, LSD and magic mushrooms estimated from these surveys is assumed to be recreational. Despite some indication of a very small amount of non-problematic opiate use, there is no real evidence as to its nature and extent, and therefore all opiate use estimated from such surveys is assumed to be problematic. As the estimated opiate use from population surveys is so small, this does not significantly impact on the estimates of the numbers of drug users in this group. However, there is evidence that cocaine use, while associated with problem drug use, is also used recreationally. One assumption, following evidence from BCS (Ramsey *et al.*, 2001), is that 50 per cent of users are problematic and 50 per cent are not, for estimates of both young recreational and older regular users. These assumptions may need to be revised in the light of future evidence.

Young recreational users include all young people aged 11 to 24. Estimates for school age young people are based on 1998 England data (Goddard and Higgins, 1999); school data for Wales in 1998 includes only young people aged 15. School surveys undertaken in England and in Wales in 2000 sample 11 to 15 year olds, but results of these surveys were not made available to us. Preliminary results are not detailed enough for our purpose (Boreham and Shaw, 2001).

Population estimates for recreational drug use among young people for England and Wales are shown in Table 2.1. The estimates presented are based on the assumption that the use of all opiates is problematic, and that half of cocaine use is problematic. Higher estimates are obtained by figures given for the use of any drug in the 'last year' and lower estimates by the use of the 'last month' figures. Estimates are based upon actual percentages from the survey data supplied to the project rather than rounded-up published percentages.

Table 2.1: Prevalence of recreational drug users amongst young people under 25

	Last year	Last month
LSD	235,000	137,000
Magic mushrooms	562,000	28,000
Ecstasy	781,000	384,000
Cocaine*	199,000	27,000
Any of above	798,000	399,000

Source: Data analysis taken from original surveys, Ramsey *et al.*, 2001; Goddard and Higgins, 1999.
Note: * assumes 50% is problematic therefore only, half of cocaine use prevalence is estimated as recreational.

Based on this table the following estimates are for the total number of young recreational users:

Number of young recreational users of Class A drugs:
399,000 (lowest estimate)
798,000 (highest estimate)

An alternative method would be to make assumptions from the 1998 Youth Lifestyle Survey (YLS), reported in At the Margins (Goulden and Sondhi, 2001). This survey asks about regularity of drug use, establishing a more refined definition of regular use, reporting on use:

- once or twice this year;
- once every couple of months;
- once a month;
- two or three times a month;
- once or twice a week;
- three to five days a week; and
- everyday.

Such data would be nearer the desired definition by type of user rather than based as a proxy on type of drug use. However, numbers from this survey are extremely small (19 reporting use of crack, 23 use of heroin and nine use of methadone in last year) and estimation based upon this evidence must be treated with extreme caution.

Using these categories it seems sensible to suggest that amongst 12–30-year-olds those who use more than once a week use problematically, that is:

- 7 per cent of cocaine users;
- 13 per cent of crack users;
- 51 per cent of heroin users; and
- 40 per cent of methadone users.

On the basis of this survey it could be assumed that some crack use is not problematic and a much smaller proportion of cocaine use is problematic. Just over half of heroin use is problematic. A major problem here however might be that data are skewed with the inclusion of very young users, and might be more precisely extrapolated for those over 15. For the basis of this exercise we have therefore not based assumptions on this evidence, but suggest this may provide a more precise estimate for future use of the model if questions on frequency of use are incorporated into larger population and school-based surveys.

High risk groups among young people

There is compelling evidence that a small but significant minority of young people, particularly those with a variety of specific domestic and social disadvantages, are more likely to use drugs, to use them more often and to consume more. In this model they are therefore likely to form a specific sub-section of young recreational users at high risk of moving into problem drug use. Specific estimates of numbers, or the patterns of causality between problems and drug use, are currently hard to come by.

The high-risk groups for whom any estimates in terms of numbers can be made are: the homeless, those in care, young offenders and truants and excludees. Information in terms of numbers about other groups – those with drug-using families and comorbidity are not available.

- Number of homeless young people: 12,400 drift in and out of sleeping rough in any year.

- Number of young people in care: approximately 50,000 young people are 'looked' after' at any time.
- Number of young offenders: YLS estimates that eight per cent of people aged 12 to 30 are serious or persistent offenders. This translates, in population terms, to 1,038,272 for this age group.
- Truants and excludees: at least one million young people truant, 13,000 are permanently excluded and 100,000 are temporarily excluded.

While there is evidence of higher prevalence of recreational drug use amongst at risk groups, evidence of 'added' use of Class A drugs is limited. Estimates of added use are based on evidence from *At The Margins* (Goulden and Sondhi, 2001); this provides information on use of drugs amongst high-risk groups in the last year. Based on this information the following estimates are made:

- 12,400 drift in and out of sleeping rough in any year. Based on 'rough sleepers', it is suggested that there is no difference in use of cocaine and ecstasy, but for:
  - LSD: 2.5 times more likely (rough sleepers 5% never homeless 2%);
  - Magic mushrooms: at least 11.3 times more likely (rough sleepers 11%: never homeless 3%).

- Extrapolating from this, approximately 620 use LSD and approximately 1,364 young 'rough sleepers' use magic mushrooms.

- Approximately 50,000 young people are 'looked after' at any time. At the Margins could not identify these young people in the YLS.

- *At the Margins* estimates that eight per cent of people aged 12 to 30 are serious or persistent offenders, this translates, in population terms, to 1,038,272 for this age group.
  - Cocaine: at least 13 times more likely (serious offenders 13%: non-offenders less than 1%);
  - Ecstasy: at least 12 times more likely (serious offenders 12%: non-offenders less than 1%);
  - LSD: at least 16 times more likely (serious offenders 8%: non-offenders less than 0.5%);
  - Magic mushrooms: at least 12 times more likely (serious offenders 6%: non-offenders less than 0.5%).

- Extrapolating from this it is estimated that amongst young offenders age 12 to 30:
  - 134,975 use cocaine; based upon assumptions that half of this will be recreational, we assume 67,488 use cocaine recreationally;
  - 124,593 use ecstasy recreationally;
  - 83,061 use LSD;
  - 62,296 use magic mushrooms.

- At least one million young people truant. Based on 12 to 16-year-olds estimates are:
  - Cocaine: at least 4 times more likely (truants 2%: non-truant less than 0.5%);
  - Ecstasy: at least 4 times more likely (truants 2%: non-truant less than 0.5%);
  - LSD: at least 8 times more likely (truants 4%: non-truant less than 0.5%);
  - Magic mushrooms: at least 10 times more likely (truants 5%: non-truant less than 0.5%).

- Extrapolating from this, it is estimated that amongst truants aged 12 to 16 years 20,000 use cocaine. Assuming half use is recreational we estimate:
  - 10,000 truants use cocaine recreationally;
  - 20,000 use ecstasy:
  - 40,000 use LSD; and
  - 50,000 use magic mushrooms.

- 13,000 are permanently excluded from school and 100,000 are temporarily excluded. Estimates are for temporary exclusions only. Amongst excludees:
  - Cocaine: at least 6 times more likely (excludees 3%: non-excludees less than 0.5%);
  - Ecstasy: At least 10 times more likely (excludees 5%: non-excludees less than 0.5%);
  - LSD: at least 14 times more likely (excludees 7%: non-excludees less than 0.5%);
  - Magic mushrooms: at least 16 times more likely (excludees 8%: non-excludees truant less than 0.5%).

- Extrapolating from this it is estimated that amongst excludes, 3,000 use cocaine. Assuming half use is recreational, we estimate that 1,500 truants use cocaine recreationally:
  - 5,000 use ecstasy;
  - 7,000 use LSD; and
  - 8,000 use magic mushrooms.

These estimates are provided to give some insight into the high-risk groups. However, no data or models could be identified to use these estimates in the costing model.

Older regular users

Given the lack of data from the population surveys, it was necessary to define older regular users in terms of the drug used rather than actual pattern of use in a similar way to that adopted in estimating young recreational users. Opiate use and crack use amongst persons over 25 from such surveys are assumed to be problematic, but as with younger recreational users, only half cocaine use is so assumed. In Table 2.2 estimates of the numbers of older regular users based upon this assumption are presented. The numbers are based upon extrapolation from the 2000 BCS and 2000 population estimates (Ramsey et al., 2001; National Statistics, 2001).

Table 2.2: Older regular users

	Last year	Last month
LSD	1,271,000	708,000
Magic mushrooms	1,609,000	804,000
Ecstasy	938,000	218,000
Cocaine*	545,000	148,000
Any of the above	2,182,000	1,091,000

Source: Data analysis taken from original survey, Ramsey et al., 2001; Goddard and Higgins, 1999.
Note: * assumes 50% is problematic, therefore only half of cocaine use prevalence is estimated as recreational.

Based on the above the following estimates are for the total number of older regular users:

Number of older regular users of Class A drugs:
1,091,000 (lowest estimate)
2,182,000 (highest estimate)

Conclusions

The estimate of the number of users is a key component of the costing model. It had been expected that a total number of users could be estimated from population surveys and problem drug users estimated using a variety of modelling techniques. The difference between the total estimate and that of problem drug users would then have yielded the total non-problematic users: younger recreational users and older regular users. In practice, the estimates of problem drug users, even using the most conservative assumptions, were larger than the population estimates from general surveys for specific Class A drugs. It was therefore necessary to define the younger recreational users and older regular users from population surveys by drug use, that is all possible problem drug users captured in the survey were excluded from the estimate. This is likely to lead to an underestimate of these two groups of drug users.

High and low estimates were calculated for young recreational users and older problem users. Three estimates were made of problem drug users. These could be combined in a number of ways to estimate the total number of Class A drug users for England and Wales for 2000. The low estimate was taken as the low estimate of all three groups giving an estimate of 1.77 million users. The high estimate is similarly estimated at 3.49 million users. One medium estimate would be to take a midpoint between these figures but this would lose the link with the specific estimates. The medium estimate was therefore taken as the conservative estimate of the low figure of the young recreational and older regular users, and the medium estimate of problem users which, at 1.82 million users, is only slightly higher than the low total estimate. However, this total estimate is not used as a key figure in estimating costs as the consequences are estimated separately for the different drug using groups. In the rest of the study the medium figure is generally used to provide the main estimate of drug related consequences. A larger range of estimates from varying the assumptions could be used in the model simulations, but there is little other evidence to guide such variations. The high, low and medium estimates given here are used as a means to illustrate how estimates may vary with estimates of the numbers of users.

Assumptions log

For each chapter a log of the main assumptions is presented. In estimating prevalence the assumptions taken from a number of published sources are:

- The duration of problem use to entry into treatment is five years.
- New episodes represent a third of those in treatment.
- Treatment coverage of problem drug use is between a third and a half.
- All use of opiates and crack is problematic, only half cocaine use is problematic.
- Estimates of problem Class A drug use prevalence are based upon modelling techniques identified by EDMMA.
- 80 per cent of Class A problem drug users have or continue to inject.

- 59 per cent of ever injectors are current injectors and 41 per cent are past injectors.
- Young recreational use is distinguished from regular use by age, the latter represented by those 25 years and older.
- Recreational use is distinguished from problem drug use.
- Recreational use cannot necessarily be defined by drug type.
- All ecstasy, LSD and magic mushroom use is recreational.
- Half of cocaine use is recreational.

Research and additional data required to improve estimates

- Attempts to estimate prevalence of drug use, for costing with respect to consequences, have highlighted a number of weaknesses in current evidence.

- A major problem is with definitions of recreational, regular and problem use, or rather the lack of information on regularity of use amongst users. Use of drugs, 'ever', in 'last year', and in 'last month' provide little understanding as to the nature of drug use, failing to provide a distinction between experimental, one-off trying, occasional and regular sustained use as part of lifestyle. While 'last month' use is commonly used as a proxy for regular use, it cannot truly be seen to represent this behaviour. The YLS style of questioning with respect to regularity of use would be more helpful in providing insight into not only problem and persistent use but also transitions from recreational to problem use. Much of this research requires longitudinal cohorts.

- Injecting of drugs is associated with major health, and long-term cost consequences; large-scale surveys used to estimate prevalence have not asked respondents about administration of drugs. Also, much of the literature on problem drug use fails to distinguish between injecting and non-injecting use. There are several other issues including poly-drug user and alcohol use within the drug using population.

- The transition process between different types of drug use – experimental to recreational to regular and finally to problem drug use – is under-researched, leading to a number of unsustainable assumptions about drug use and its consequences. The issues around use of cocaine have been highlighted above.

- Opiate use again is assumed to be associated with problem drug use, though it is reported by a small proportion of young users, including those as young as 11; indeed, prevalence amongst young people aged 11 to 15 for 'last year' use is as high as for 16 to 24-year-olds. The nature of this use – whether it is experimental, occasional or regular, or the problems associated with it – is not well understood. Similarly with older users, there is little understanding of the use of opiates and cocaine as recreational drugs.

- To provide better evidence of number of years of drug use before entering treatment, it is recommended that this information be provided through treatment monitoring systems.

- Estimates of prevalence are crucial not only to the methodology proposed in this report but to all other costing models. More particularly, if costs are to be monitored over time through successive CSR exercises, it becomes very important to be able to constantly monitor changes in prevalence over time.

3. Estimating the cost consequences

Introduction

The aim of this chapter is to examine the consequences of Class A drug use in England and Wales for the year 2000. Consequences were considered for all types of users.

Table 1.1 gives a starting point to consider different consequences. The main domains for costs are health, work, driving, crime and other economic and social impacts. In practice, however, there are limited data to estimate these effects. Also even when there are some known and measured consequences there may be difficulties in assigning values for some concepts.

In the following sections the available estimates are presented for the different groups of users. Where possible, ranges of figures are presented along with estimates per user.

Young recreational users

As reviewed in the previous project (Culyer *et al.*, 2002) most consequences of drug use are not available in the form of the risk probabilities, given the level of use. For young recreational users the data are available simply on the current level of consequences. Figures are therefore based on data such as the current level of Class A drug-related deaths. This implies that the higher the current estimate of use the lower the estimate of the cost per user.

Health

Young recreational users are at risk from toxicity and overdose which exceptionally lead to death. Such deaths have public finance consequences (health care use) and obviously involve a social loss (the additional health resources and the years of life lost). There are additional health care consequences from toxicity and overdose that do not result in mortality.

It is assumed that any death reported related to cocaine use from those aged under 25 should be attributed to problem use. Twenty deaths from ecstasy were reported by coroners in 2000 (Pollard, 2001). It is difficult to know whether some deaths from ecstasy or other Class A drugs by young recreational users are not identified through the current system. The estimated number of young people taking ecstasy in 2000 was between 384,000 and 781,000 (Chapter 2).

This information is on an observed consequence, ecstasy-related deaths, rather than as suggested being in the form of a risk relationship. This means that in terms of the consequences only one estimate is available.

There are a number of issues that arise in putting a value on the loss of life in this way. For this project, estimates of the costs of deaths are based on those used for valuing road traffic accidents (Department of the Environment, Transport and the Regions (DETR), 1999). These values were gathered using a variety of methods and divided between the medical and ambulance costs; a lost output calculation and the human cost. The estimate of lost output is calculated as the present value of the expected loss of earnings plus any non-wage payments (national insurance contributions etc.) paid by the employer. The human cost element is based on the average population willingness to pay to avoid the risk of death. This figure was derived from a literature survey of such values. Including both a human cost and lost output elements for a death is debatable. Also, other elements could be valued in this type of calculation, for example, saving in the lifetime health care costs of those in this group who may have developed problem use. There are little data, however, to make such calculations or adjustments for this group of currently young recreational users. The DETR value of life was therefore used as an example of a value currently used in policy decisions.

Current valuation gives an estimate of £670 for the medical and ambulance costs; £750,640 for the human costs and £393,580 for the lost output component. The £670 element relates to health care costs of a road traffic accident death. It is unclear whether an ecstasy-related death would be more or less expensive and this figure is used in the absence of other estimates. The total social cost of each death is £1,144,890 in 2000 prices. This yields the following estimates:

Health service costs of ecstasy deaths in 2000: £13,000
Other social costs of ecstasy deaths in 2000: £22,884,400

These figures can also be expressed in terms of the cost per user. Given the estimate of 384,000 users, this would yield a health service cost of £0.03 per user and a total social cost (health resource and other social costs) of £59.59 per user. Obviously, because the consequences have been calculated from an observed figure, using the higher number of estimated ecstasy users of 781,000 yields a lower estimate of the cost per user of £0.017 and £29.30 respectively.

All recreational drug users may be at some risk from drug-related health problems, particularly toxicity and overdose. As reviewed in Culyer *et al.* (2002), there are no epidemiological studies giving risks for a range of medical conditions. The only available information is for recorded hospital episodes. There were 136 bed days from 26 episodes from any poisoning by narcotics and psychotics for individuals aged under 25 in England in the year 1999-2000 (Department of Health, 2001b). These admissions were all for LSD and have therefore been attributed to young recreational use rather than problem use. These figures seem low and may underestimate hospital use, especially Accident and Emergency Admissions. No data were available to check these estimates.

These episodes can be valued as follows. Each episode (26 were recorded) is likely to involve some ambulance costs and admission through Accident and Emergency Departments (A&E) as well as the cost per bed day for each of the 136 days recorded. The ambulance costs were taken at £179 per episode and an A&E admission of £65 per episode (figures taken from Netten and Curtis, 2000). The bed day costs are based on the average costs per day of inpatient episodes for poisoning, toxic effects and overdose of £226 (NHS Schedule of Reference Costs, 2000). The total cost for the 26 episodes and 136 bed days is therefore £37,080.

The only other hospital admissions directly related to young recreational users are for mental illness, see Table 3.1. Admissions were not available delineated by age. The drug-related mental illness admissions were therefore allocated 50 per cent to young recreational users and 50 per cent to older regular users.

Table 3.1: *Mental health admissions related to young recreational drug use*

Type of episode	No.	Bed days
Mental and behavioural disorders due to sedatives and hypnotics:		
Psychotic disorder	8	195
Residual and late-onset psychotic disorder	2	60
Mental and behavioural disorders due to multiple /psychoactive drugs		
Psychotic disorder	428	13,696
Amnesic syndrome	3	314
Residual and late-onset psychotic disorder	6	198
Total	447	14,463

Source: Department of Health, 2001b.

These bed days can be valued at £146 per day (Netten and Curtis, 2000). This gives a total cost of £2,111,598 for England.

Summing all the available health service costs for young recreational users gives an estimate of £2,161,678 (£13,000 + £37,080 + £2,111,598). Available data only cover hospital expenditure and there is no evidence about any excess use of primary care. Data are only available where drug use has been identified as a cause and the episode has been coded. This may be an underestimate of the total impact of recreational drug use. Also, data on hospital use were only available for England and exclude any impact in Wales.

The summary health effects for young recreational users per year are:

Health Service Costs (Reactive government expenditure): £2,161,678
Total Social Costs in the Health Domain: £25,046,078

Work

Part of the valuation of ecstasy-related deaths includes an element for lost productivity from that death. There are also likely to be some productivity effects from drug use by young recreational users. This may be short-term increasing sickness absence or affecting performance at work. There may also be longer-term impacts for the individual if drug use has impacted on education or employment history. There is no evidence that recreational use by under 25s is associated with unemployment. There is evidence of a causal association between productivity loss and drug use but no data are available to estimate these effects.

Driving

There are studies which suggest recreational drug users drive having recently consumed drugs. One recent study of use by clubbers suggests that 43 per cent had used ecstasy, 25 per cent cocaine and eight per cent LSD and also driven (Ingram et al., 2001). Applying these percentages to all young recreational users would yield the following estimates:

Use of ecstasy prior to driving:
165,120 (lowest estimate)
335,830 (highest estimate)

Use of cocaine prior to driving:
67,200 (lowest estimate)
796,000 (highest estimate)

Use of LSD prior to driving:
10,960 (lowest estimate)
18,800 (highest estimate)

However, these figures are based on one survey of clubbers and it is unclear whether or not such proportions would translate to the whole recreational drug using group. The figures are therefore only given as an illustration of the potential size of the population with this risk.

While there is evidence of driver fatalities having tested positive for drugs (18% tested positive, Department of Environment, Transport and the Regions, 1999) this cannot assume that such tests are causally linked to the traffic accidents. Further research is required before any risk from the incidence of taking drugs recreationally and driving accidents can be calculated.

Crime
There are two major crime elements considered for this group: acquisitive crime; and crimes associated with possession of recreational drugs. There is no evidence of a causal relationship between acquisitive crime and younger recreational drug use. It may be part of the transition between young recreational users and problem users that use increases to a point where some acquisitive crime is conducted.

The numbers of drug possession offences depend on the level of police activity. Any changes in policy will impact on the criminal justice costs. What is currently impossible to determine is the impact of such enforcement expenditure on the level of drug use and other drug consequences. It is difficult to determine in the context of the model whether the drug possession criminal justice costs should be classed as proactive or reactive. They are included in this section as a reactive cost. Individual drug users may suffer other costs if they have a criminal conviction. Such costs have not been included in this report.

Data on those arrested for possession are broken down by substance but not by age. It is assumed that half the arrests for possession are among the under 25s. All such arrests for ecstasy and LSD are assumed to be attributable to young recreational users. For the estimated cocaine arrests, one half are assumed to be young recreational users and one half to be young problem users. Using the latest available data from the Home Office (relating to 1998) this yields an estimate of:

- 1,560 arrests for ecstasy use
- 306 arrests for LSD
- 1,112 arrests for cocaine
- 2,798 total arrests

An estimate of the costs of a drug possession arrest can be derived from figures reported in Brand and Price (2000). An estimate of £3,551 per arrest was calculated based on the total police costs for drug-related offences from Brand and Price (2000) divided by the total number of drug offences (Corkery, 2001). However, these figures related to a mixture of possession and supply offences and it is likely that for young recreational and older regular users these arrests are generally for possession. Therefore, a more general cost of arrest of £1,346 was used. This figure is based on police expenditure and all arrests allowing for other police activities (see Godfrey *et al.*, 2002).

Estimated costs for drug possession arrests for young recreational users: £3,766,108

Other social consequences

No other social consequences were identified for young recreational users.

High-risk groups

Among the high-risk group within young recreational users the consumption of Class A drugs may well be higher than among the rest of this group. There are no estimated additional costs, either in reactive government expenditure or wider social costs for this group.

Older regular users

Categories of costs for older regular Class A drug users are very similar to those already described for younger recreational users.

Health

There is no evidence of ecstasy death amongst older users. Without evidence to the contrary, cocaine deaths are assumed to be associated with problem use.

Reported hospital episodes due to poisoning and intoxication are, however, higher for older users than among young people. As with younger recreational users, data are only available for England. The number of episodes and bed days taken from Department of Health (2001b) are shown in Table 3.2.

Table 3.2: Hospital episodes for those aged over 25 years

Hospital episode data for 1999-2000 shows the following FCE for over 25 year olds:

Type of episode	No.	Bed days
Poisoning by LSD	17	10
Poisoning by cocaine	221	1,017
Total	238	1,027

Using the same estimates of costs this yields: 238 times £179 for ambulance costs; 238 times £65 for A&E costs; and 1027 times £226 for the cost of bed days. The total is £290,174.

The data for drug-related, mental illness admissions were not available by age. These admissions were therefore divided between the older regular and younger recreational users. The number of episodes and bed days for this group is therefore assumed to be the same as in Table 3.1.

Using a unit cost of £146 per bed day (Netten and Curtis, 2000) as before, the health care costs can be calculated as £2,111,598.

Total health service use among older regular users is costed as £2,401,800 per year. This figure excludes any primary care costs for this group. The summary health-care costs identified can therefore be summarised as:

Total health care costs for older regular users: £2,401,800

Work

There is no evidence that recreational use of Class A drugs by older users is associated with unemployment. There is some evidence of a causal link between recreational drug use and productivity losses but no data are available in the UK to estimate these impacts.

Driving

Based on the same study as used for younger recreational users (Ingram *et al.*, 2001), the following estimates can be made of the numbers of older regular users who drive after taking drugs. Given the limited nature of this survey as previously mentioned, these figures are given as an illustration of the potential size of the risk population.

Use of ecstasy prior to driving:
93,740 (lowest estimate) (43% of 218,000)
403,304 (highest estimate) (43% of 938,000)

Use of cocaine prior to driving:
37,000 (lowest estimate) (25% of 148,000)
136,250 (highest estimate) (25% of 545,000)

Use of LSD prior to driving:
56,640 (lowest estimate) (8% of 708,000)
101,680 (highest estimate) (8% of 1,271,000)

There are currently no data to translate the incidence of drug-driving into adverse consequences.

Crime

There is no evidence of a causal relationship between acquisitive crime and Class A regular use. There are data on drug possession arrests and, as with younger users, the size of this consequence depends on policing policies. As with younger users, this expenditure is classified for this project as a reactive expenditure.

The number of offences was assumed to be split equally between the younger recreational and older regular users group. The number of offences is therefore estimated at the same level as for younger recreational users, yielding a cost estimate of £3,776,108.

Other social costs

No other social costs were identified for older regular users.

Problem drug users and treatment related consequences

It is known that problem drug users have a range of problems that impact on a range of people in society. It is also clear from research evidence that the level of these consequences is lower on average for those drug users in treatment than for those out of treatment. This division is also important to make as the active scenario arrest referral is assumed to act on consequences through attracting more people into treatment. However, research on those in treatment suggest that most drug users in the UK have a number of periods in and out of treatment (Gossop *et al.*, 2001; Coid *et al.*, 2000). Therefore treatment cannot be treated simply as a one-off event with a clear pattern of before and after the event costs. There will also be those who have never been in a treatment programme. Given that they may have a shorter drug-using career, these users may be expected to have accumulated fewer adverse effects. On the other hand, these users may be more chaotic and therefore have very high levels of problems.

Research is limited, but it could be assumed that a third of problem users are in treatment, a third have previously been in treatment and a third have never been in treatment (Frischer *et al.*, 2001). However, these are broad assumptions based mainly on observational data and expert opinion. These proportions were used in this simulation as a starting point, but this is a major area for further research. Further divisions could be made. For example, assuming that two-thirds of those never in treatment are relatively young and may suffer fewer consequences than others as a result of their drug use. Of this sub-group one half may become drug-free without help, but the other half may need some help from an agency. The remaining third of those never in treatment may well be chaotic. These illustrative proportions are illustrated in Table 3.3.

Table 3.3: Assumed treatment status of current problem drug users

In treatment (a third)	Not in treatment (two thirds)			
	Previously in treatment (a third)	Never in treatment (a third)		
		Less consequences (2 in 9)		Chaotic (1 in 9)
		May require treatment (1 in 9)	Recover without help (1 in 9)	

Ideally, health, work, driving, crime and other social consequences could be attributed to users in these different treatment states. In reality data are not available which are related in such detail to the user's treatment history. It was therefore not possible to use this detailed type of division in this project.

The main source of data for the consequences of problem drug users used in this research has been taken from the National Treatment Outcome Research Study (NTORS), Gossop et al. (1996). This study, funded by the Department of Health, consists of a cohort study of 1,075 drug users entering treatment in 1995. The study used a large number of providers spread throughout England, but there was no sampling basis to ensure those attenders were representative of the total population of those attending treatment in that year. Also, there may have been changes in the population coming forward for treatment in the subsequent periods and changes in the treatment received. However, the findings of NTORS have been found to be similar to comparable US and UK studies (Coid et al., 2000; Gossop et al., 2001). These NTORS patients were asked about a number of consequences before entering treatment and one year and two years after treatment. A further longer-term follow-up has just been completed, which confirms the treatment outcome data, but no economic analysis has been undertaken on the five-year follow-up data.

Data from special analysis of this study and based on the methodology used in economic analysis of the baseline, one-year and two-year follow-up data from the survey (Godfrey et al., 2002) are used in this report. For the analysis, the groups from Table 3.3 were collapsed into two groups: those currently in treatment (one-third) and those not currently in treatment (two-thirds), taken from Frischer et al., 2001. It was assumed that those not in treatment had experiences closely related to the consequences of NTORS participants in the twelve months before entering treatment. Those in treatment were assumed to have the level of consequences experienced from the community treatment programmes (methadone programmes). New treatment attenders are assumed to have the levels of consequences recorded at the one-year follow-up point. Those who are assumed to be treatment attenders for longer than one year are assumed to have the levels of consequences recorded at the two-year follow-up point. It should be noted at the follow-up period that not all the individuals are assumed to have remained in the same treatment programme for that period. Also, the two-thirds majority classified as "not in treatment" would have experienced some addiction-related treatment in the previous two years. Clearly, further research is needed to relate costs to different treatment status to improve the accuracy of this model. The figures for the numbers of problem users in these three groups based on the medium estimate of problem drug users of 337,350 are shown in Table 3.4.

Table 3.4: **Number of problem users by group, medium estimate**

	Not in treatment	In treatment	
		<1 year	> 1 year
Number	224,900	56,225	56,225

Consequences of problem drug users related to treatment are dealt with under the headings: health; criminal justice costs; work (benefit income) and other social consequences arising from crime. There were no data on drug use and driving collected as part of this study. Further costs of problem drug use relating to deaths; neonatal care; children in care; deaths and other effects of methadone poisoning in children in drug-using families are considered separately. Figures are presented on the additional costs related to injecting drug users although these are not, because of potential double counting, added to the total cost estimates.

Health service use consequences of problem users in and out of drug treatment

The NTORS study asked individual drug users for their use of a range of health services including visits to the GP (other than to collect scripts); A&E attendances; inpatient stays for physical health problems (excluding addiction treatment); outpatient mental health-care and inpatient mental health-care stays. The responses related to the total NHS resource use of the drug user (excluding addiction treatment) and no attempt was made to ask individuals the proportion of this use which was related to drug use rather than other health issues. The figures for health service consequences could therefore be seen as an overestimate of health service costs relating to drug use. However, the estimates only relate to current health service use and do not make any adjustment for the impact of current drug use on future health-care demands. An alternative method would be to attempt to identify specific drug-related illness from treatment samples or routine data sources. However, no suitable sources of data were found. All figures are presented in detail using the medium estimates of problem drug users for clarity, with the high and low estimates being presented as totals to illustrate the sensitivity of figures to the estimate of the size of the problem drug-using group.

The data from the NTORS study for different types of health service use are considered in turn. Of those in treatment, 50 per cent are presumed to have started the treatment within the year and therefore data from the one-year follow-up point is used for this group of problem drug users. The other 50 per cent are presumed to have experienced a number of treatments over a longer period and therefore the two-year follow-up data is used for this group. No data (or literature) were found to support this split and some limited sensitivity analysis is undertaken to test the importance of this division. An alternative would be to make no distinction and use some average outcome figure. However, differences year to year in treatment outcomes could have a significant impact on different elements of the public sector. It was felt this refinement did add a useful dimension to the model, especially for the planned simulations of arrest referral and other policies where the impact was to alter the numbers of new entrants into treatment. A further assumption is that the results at the two-year point continue beyond the two-year period. However, this assumption has more empirical support in that the initial analysis of the five-year NTORS study outcomes suggest most outcomes have remained relatively stable between the two-and five-year follow-up points (Gossop *et al.*, 2001).

The *primary care* visits are taken as follows:

- 3.6 GP visits per user not in treatment
- 5.6 GP visits per user starting treatment within the year
- 6.8 GP visits per user in treatment system over one year

Using these figures, this translates into the following numbers of GP visits per year: 809,640 visits among the group not in treatment; 314,860 among those in treatment for less than one year; and 383,330 for those in treatment for more than one year. It should be noted these are estimated visits over and above any visits associated with their treatment for drug misuse.

These estimates of numbers of visits were combined with the estimate of cost per visit to the GP of £18 (Netten and Curtis, 2000). This yields the calculation of costs per year of: £14,573,520 for those not in treatment; £5, 667,480 for those in treatment less than one year; and £6,881,940 for those in treatment over one year. This yields a total of £27.1 million using the medium estimate of problem drug users. The range of estimates for GP use by drug users is between £23.0 million (low estimate) and £40.7 million (high estimate).

For *A&E* use, the following data were used:

- 0.7 episodes per user not in treatment. This figure is similar to the estimate of 23 per cent reporting they had an accidental overdose in the year prior to treatment (Coid *et al.*, 2000)
- 0.8 episodes per user in treatment for less than one year
- 0.8 episodes per user in treatment for more than one year

Applying these figures to the numbers in the different groups yields the number of A&E visits each year as: 157,430 for those not in treatment; 44,980 for those in treatment for less than one year; and 44,980 for those in treatment for more than one year.

It was assumed that many of these visits would be of a serious kind, often involving an overdose incident and therefore a cost of £282 per visit was used (Netten and Curtis (2000). This value assumes an overnight stay. No questions were asked in the survey about emergency ambulance use and therefore this value is likely to be a reasonable estimate of overall NHS costs, even if some visits were shorter than overnight. The estimated costs are: £44,395,260 for those not in treatment; £12,684,360 for those in treatment less than one year; and £12,684,360 for those in treatment more than one year. The total cost is therefore estimated at £69.8 million using the medium estimate of the number of problem drug users, varying between £58 million and £105 million using the lower and higher estimates.

The *inpatient hospital* stays were assumed as follows:

- 1.75 days per user not in treatment
- 2.8 days per user in treatment less than one year
- 2.4 days per user in treatment more than one year

These figures translate to the numbers of bed days being: 393,575 for those not in treatment; 157,430 for those in treatment less than one year and 134,940 for those in treatment for more than one year.

The costs were taken at £223 per day (Netten and Curtis, 2000). This yields an estimate of £87,767,225 for those not in treatment; £35,106,890 for those in treatment less than one year and £30,091,620 for those in treatment for more than one year. The total figure is estimated at £153.0 million, varying between £127 million and £229 million.

Participants in the NTORS study were also asked about their use of mental health services. The analysis from that study using the intake, one-year and two-year follow-up data, yielded the following figures for community mental health service use:

- 1.3 outpatient mental health visits per user not in treatment
- 0.8 outpatient mental health visits per user in treatment less than one year
- 1.6 outpatient mental health visits per user in treatment more than one year

This yields the total estimated number of community mental health visits of: 292,370 for those not in treatment; 44,980 for those in treatment less than one year and 89,980 for those in treatment of more than one year.

Costs of community treatment for psychological or emotional problems are estimated at £50 per visit (Netten and Curtis, 2000). This may be an underestimate of the value as some of these visits may be more expensive outpatient visits to a psychiatrist. With no additional information however, the lower estimate of visits within the community were taken. The costs are estimated as: £14,618,500 for those not in treatment, £2,249,000 for those in treatment less than one year and £4,498,000 for those in treatment more than one year. The total across all groups is estimated at £21.4 million, varying between £17.8 million and £32.0 million.

Extrapolating from NTORS estimates of the number of drug users receiving inpatient mental health treatment (excluding addiction treatments) are:

- 1.5 days per user not in treatment
- 0.4 days per user in treatment less than one year
- 2 days per user in treatment more than one year

Using these figures, the estimate of the number of mental health bed days used by problem drug users each year is 337,350 for those not in treatment, 22,490 for those in treatment less than one year and 112,450 for those in treatment for more than one year.

Costs are estimated at £144 per day (Netten and Curtis, 2000). Applying this unit cost figure to the estimated numbers of mental health inpatient bed days yields estimates of costs of: £48,578,400 for those not in treatment, £3,238,560 for those in treatment less than one year and £16,192,800 for those in treatment more than one year.

Table 3.5: Health service costs (£) for problem drug users 2000

Type of health cost	Not in treatment	In treatment	
		<1 year	>1 year
Primary care	£14,573,520	£5,667,480	£6,881,940
A&E	£44,395,260	£12,684,360	£12,684,360
Inpatient care	£87,767,225	£35,106,890	£30,091,620
Community mental health	£14,618,500	£2,249,000	£4,498,000
Inpatient mental health	£48,578,400	£3,238,560	£16,192,800
TOTAL	£209,932,905	£58,946,290	£70,348,720

These different elements of health service cost are summarised in Table 3.5. Problem drug users are estimated to cost the health service between £283 million and £509 million per year, in addition to the specific addiction treatment they may be receiving. This addiction treatment is treated as proactive government spending within the costing model. This figure also excludes additional costs from infectious disease risks among injecting drug users.

Table 3.6: Summary health care expenditure per year £ million, 2000

	Not in treatment	In treatment		TOTAL
		< 1 year	> 1 year	
Low	175.4	49.1	58.6	283
Medium	209.9	58.0	70.3	339
High	314.9	88.4	105.5	509

The total sum can also be expressed as a cost per user, approximately £1,000. The average is similar whether high, low or medium estimates are used, given the methods used to calculate these figures which use the same estimate of effect per user. There are differences, however, in the costs per user across treatment status, £933 for those not in treatment, £1,048 for those in treatment under one year and £1,251 for those in treatment more than one year. It may seem surprising that health expenditure per user seems higher for those engaged in treatment than those not in treatment. This may reflect the poor health state of problem drug users and escalating health problems or, indeed, some deficit of health-care needs which are picked up and dealt with while the user is engaged in treatment. Further five-year data from the NTORS study are needed to examine whether health-care utilisation falls in future years. These findings do imply that increasing the number of problem drug users into treatment may increase reactive health-care expenditure at least in the short-term.

Work

It is known that problem drug users have problems with maintaining employment in the legitimate economy. The data from the NTORS study suggested that, among the cohort prior to intake, 81 per cent were mostly unemployed. As with crime, the link between drug use and employment is likely to be complex with, for some, unemployment being a causal factor for drug use rather than drug use being a causal factor for unemployment. There are no data to separate these impacts. Among those entering community-based treatments, the numbers unemployed fell slightly to 79 per cent and the same number were mostly unemployed at the two-year follow-up point. That is the change in employment is small. Estimates are again taken from the NTORS study with data prior to intake figures being taken for problem users not in treatment, the one year follow up figures for the community treatment being taken for those engaging in treatment in the year in question, and the two year follow-up being used for those problem drug users engaged in treatment for more than a year. The estimated numbers receiving state benefits are given in Table 3.7.

Unemployment clearly has implications for government reactive expenditure. Full benefit entitlement will depend upon the family circumstances and the take-up of benefits among the problem drug users. As a minimum estimate, unemployment costs are based upon Job Seekers allowance for those over 25 at £52.20 per week; £2,714 per year (Emmersen and Lancaster, 2000). Applied to the estimates of number of problem drug users yields the estimate of government reactive benefit expenditure as shown in Table 3.7. As suggested above, however, this expenditure cannot be taken in isolation as being totally attributable to drug use.

Table 3.7:   Estimate of numbers in receipt of state benefit and expenditure

	Not in treatment	In treatment	
		<1 year	> 1 year
Numbers	182,169	44,418	44,418
Estimated cost, £, 2000	£494,406,666	£120,550,452	£120,550,452

The resource (social cost) implications of these high levels of unemployment are harder to estimate. It could be argued that spells of long-term unemployment have life-time implications for the individual problem drug users and there is a loss of labour resource for the economy. Others suggest that the value in terms of economic loss will depend on the economic circumstances. No attempt was made in this study to estimate the wider resource consequences of the level of unemployment among problem drug users.

Crime

The relationship between crime and problem drug use is complex. However, one of the main outcomes of individuals taking up drug treatment is a fall in offending. There are two elements to the economic impact of crime. The first element is the expenditure by the criminal justice system dealing with the crimes committed (including drug offences). For some crimes and some criminal justice expenditure, e.g., prison costs, the government reactive spend may occur some time after the offence was committed. Also, the level of expenditure will depend not only on the offending rate but also the success of the CJS in apprehending and detaining offenders.

The second element of the economic costs of crime is the impact on the victims of crime. These costs can take the form of expenditures taken in anticipation of crime, for example, shop security measures or burglar alarms for homes. There are also more direct victim costs of crime in terms of material or physical damage and loss, and the wider fear of crime elements (Brand and Price, 2000).

The NTORS study has data both on direct contacts of problem drug users with the criminal justice system and self-reports of the numbers of offences committed. The two elements of the cost of drug-related crime are estimated from these data. As one purpose of this study is to estimate actual government reactive spending flow changes, CJS expenditure is based on the reported contacts. For drug users in treatment, some CJS expenditure may relate to offences committed before the user was in treatment.

The data available for directly estimating CJS expenditures are drug arrests, arrests for acquisitive crimes, stays in police custody, appearances in court and stays in prison. NTORS data suggests the following pattern *of drug arrests*:

- 0.3 arrests per user not in treatment;
- 0.8 arrests per user in treatment less than one year; and
- 0.4 arrests per user in treatment more than one year.

These figures yield estimates of the number of arrests for the problem user group as 67,470 for those not in treatment, 44,980 for those in treatment less than one year and 22,492 for those in treatment more than one year when using the medium estimate of problem users. The pattern of an increase in arrests in the first year of treatment is puzzling. The data are as supplied for the project from the NTORS data and further analyses of the results obtained was not possible within this project.

These figures are used with the estimate for the cost of a drug possession or supply arrest of £3,551 to estimate the police costs, discussed above. It should be noted that it is assumed, following Brand and Price (2000), that there are no victim costs associated with drug-related offences. This yields a cost of £239,585,970 for those problem users not in treatment, £159,723,980 for those in treatment less than one year and £79,869,092 for those in treatment more than one year.

The NTORS data are used to suggest the following pattern of arrests for acquisitive *crimes* among problem drug users:

- 1.35 arrests per drug user not in treatment in a year;
- 1.6 arrests for users in treatment for less than one year; and
- 0.4 arrest for users in treatment for more than one year.

Extrapolating from these figures gives the estimates for the number of arrests of 303,615 for those not in treatment, 89,960 for those in treatment less than one year and 22,492 arrest for those in treatment more than one year.

Arrest costs for these offences are estimated at £1,346, taking the lower more general arrest costs discussed above. This yields costs of £408,665,790 for those problem drug users not in treatment, £121,086,160 for those in treatment less than one year and £30,274,232 for those in treatment more than one year.

Based on NTORS, we estimate problem drug users are held in *police custody*, on average:

- prior to treatment, 2 nights;
- at one year, 1.2 nights; and
- at two years, 0.8 nights.

These figures translate to estimates of the number of nights in police custody as 449,800 for those not in treatment, 67,470 for those in treatment less than one year and 44,980 for those in treatment for more than one year.

Costs of overnight stays are estimated at £69 per stay (Godfrey *et al.*, 2002) and the estimated costs are £31,036,200 for those not in treatment, £4,655,430 for those in treatment less than one year and £3,103,620 for those in treatment more than one year.

The NTORS data are used to provide the following estimates of *court appearances*:

- 2.2 occasions per year for those not in treatment;
- 1.4 occasions per year for those in treatment less than one year; and
- 1.2 occasion per year for those in treatment more than one year.

This provides the estimate of the court appearances for the medium estimate of problem users as 494,780 for those not in treatment, 78,715 for those in treatment less than one year and 64,470 for those in treatment more than one year.

The costs of court appearances are estimated at £699 per appearance based on Harries (1999), yielding the estimates of criminal justice costs of £345,851,220 for those not in treatment, £55,021,785 for those in treatment less than one year and £47,161,530 for those in treatment more than one year.

Using NTORS data, it is estimated that problem drug users spend:

- 36 days in prison per year out of treatment;
- 34 days in prison per year in the first year of treatment; and
- 39 days in prison per year for those in treatment more than one year.

This yields the estimate of the number of days in *prison* of 8,096,400 for those out of treatment, 1,911,650 for those in treatment less than one year and 2,192,775 for those in treatment more than one year.

Costs per day in prison are estimated at £68.86 (Godfrey *et al.*, 2002) and this yields the estimates of prison costs for the medium estimate of the problem drug-using population of £557,518,104 for those out of treatment, £131,636,219 for those in treatment less than one year and £150,994,486 for those in treatment more than one year.

Table 3.8: *Summary of criminal justice costs (£), medium estimate of problem drug users, 2000*

	Not in treatment	In treatment	
		<1 year	> 1 year
Arrests for drug offences	239,585,970	158,723,980	79,869,092
Arrests for acquisitive crime	408,665,790	121,086,160	30,274,232
Police detention	31,036,200	4,655,430	3,103,620
Court appearances	345,851,220	55,021,785	47,161,530
Prison stays	557,518,104	131,636,219	150,994,486
TOTAL	1,582,657,284	472,123,576	311,402,960

The costs of police in terms of arrests and stays in the police cells, court appearances and prison stays give an estimate of the criminal justice costs of problem drug users by treatment status. The figures for the medium estimate of problem drug users are given by category and treatment status in Table 3.8. The total estimates by treatment status and for the different estimates of the number of problem drug users are given in Table 3.9. These costs vary from £1,972 million to £3,549 million depending on the estimates of the number of problem users. The cost per user is £701 based on the medium estimate.

Table 3.9: *Summary estimates of criminal justice costs, £ million*

	Not in treatment	In treatment		TOTAL for all problem users
		< 1year	> 1 year	
Lowest estimate	1,319.0	393.4	259.5	1,972
Medium estimate	1,582.7	472.1	311.4	2,366
Highest estimate	2,374.0	707.4	467.1	3,549

Other social costs – victim costs of crime

There are likely to be a number of other social impacts of drug use related to treatment status, including driving, for which no data are available. However, as described above there are the victim costs of crime. Using the Brand and Price (2000) estimates, and the pattern of offences self reported by NTORS clients, yields the following estimates of the wider social costs of crime:

- £30,827 per year for problem drug user not in treatment;
- £8,893 per year for problem drug user in treatment less than one year; and
- £13,464 per year for problem drug user in treatment more than one year.

These figures reflect the fall in the offences committed by NTORS clients after they had entered the treatment under study (Gossop *et al.*, 2001). Using these figures and the medium estimate of problem users, yields a total cost of £8190 million, and an estimate of £24,277 victim cost per user.

Table 3.10: Estimates of the victim costs of crime, £ million, 2000

	Not in treatment	In Treatment < 1 year	In Treatment > 1 year	TOTAL for all problem users
Lowest estimate	5,778	417	630	6,825
Medium estimate	6,933	500	757	8,190
Highest estimate	10,400	751	1,135	12,286

Other costs of problem drug users not covered in the estimates related to treatment

There are various impacts of problem drug users which are not available from the NTORS study or other treatment data. There is a high rate of premature deaths among problem drug users, and additional health and social care resources required from impacts on children and the unborn. Information on deaths is based on six-monthly figures provided by the National Programme on Substance Abuse Deaths (Ghodse *et al.*, 2001) for January to June. The full year report was not available when this research was conducted. Figures are doubled to provide estimates for the year.

Estimated deaths from opiates: 846
Estimated deaths from cocaine: 26
Total 872

Health service costs of death are estimated as £670; a total of £584,240.

Health service costs of death: £584,240
Total social costs of death: £998 million

The wider social costs of these deaths using the DETR estimate of £1,144,220 are estimated at £998 million.

In England, statistics of hospital episodes for 1999 to 2000 (Department of Health, 2001b) are shown in Table 3.11.

Table 3.11:   Neonatal effects of drug misuse 1999-00 England

	Code	FSE	Admissions	Emergency admissions	Average length of stay
Newborn babies were affected by maternal use of drugs of addiction.	P04.4	161	120	3	13
Neonatal withdrawal syndrome from maternal use of drugs of addiction.	P96.1	914	702	71	18.1

Source: Department of Health (2001b)

Following NERA (2001), costs are based on HRG N04: Neonatal Treatment with Multiple Major Diagnoses (National Schedule of Reference Costs, 2000). This gives an average cost of £4,023 per episode and the estimated cost of neonatal effects of £4,324,755. This estimate is likely to be an under-estimate as it does not include the costs of specialist clinics for pregnant drug users, midwives and health visitors.

Neonatal health service costs: £4,324,755

Amongst NTORS clients, 47 per cent had responsibility for children under 18. Some of these children may be in need of social care. In Coid *et al*'s sample, nine per cent of those who had children had, at some point, had their children taken into care or in need (at risk) (Coid *et al.*, 2000). Evidence of drug users who have children in need, but who are not looked after by local authorities, is harder to find, but one research project reported ten per cent of drug users in the care of GPs to have children on the at risk register, (Eaton, 1998). Costs of care are different for those in care from those not in care but at risk. Costs for 'looked after' children are estimated at £435 per week, or £22,650 per year (National Statistics/Department of Health, 2001). Costs of care for children in need are estimated at £85 per week, or £4,420 per year. Without better numbers of children in care, it would seem reasonable to take the figure of nine per cent of drug users with children had at least one child at risk. The minimum sum would be that this number of children is costed at £4,420 per year.

Estimates of the cost to social services of caring for children in need:
£52,560,814 (lowest estimate)
£63,072,980 (medium estimate)
£75,687,576 (highest estimate)

Statistics of hospital episodes for 1999 to 2000 (Department of Health, 2001a) show 16 cases of toxicity due to opioid use amongst children less than 15 years of age. There is no indication of whether these were the result of accidental use of parents, methadone; nor whether the parents was in treatment or not in treatment.

There is evidence that 16 young people under 15 were admitted to hospital following opiate poisoning, though there is no information as to whether this was following accidental use of parents, methadone.

In England and Wales in 2000, one child under 4 years was reported as dying following methadone poisoning.

Injecting drug users

Injecting drug users are a sub-set of problem drug users. The NTORS sample on which many of the costs of problem users were based included injecting users. It is important to avoid double counting of the same costs. Health-care costs may well therefore include health costs relating to injecting problems and even infectious diseases. What is not included is the future impacts of the spread of drug-related infections, such as HIV and Hepatitis B and C. In this section, some of the sources of data to estimate specific impacts related to injecting drug users are reviewed, but these estimates are not included in the summary figures presented in the next section.

There is an assumption that injecting drug users are at higher risk of accidental overdose and death than non-injecting drug users, though we assume a majority of episodes are accounted for by injecting drug users. With available evidence, estimates should be made on the basis of current injectors.

There is no literature evidence on the extra risk of overdose through injecting use, though we assume a majority of episodes are accounted for by injecting drug users.

Injecting of drugs is associated with a number of health problems. Coid *et al.* (2000), notes that most respondents had experienced pruritis and a quarter had sores and skin ulcers due to intravenous drug use. Fifteen per cent of clients in the NTORS study were reported to have injection-related abscesses and infections.

Based on these figures we assume (the mean of 15% and 25%) 20 per cent of injecting drug users with injecting site abscess and infections. Estimates are based on current injectors, as estimated in Chapter 2, and shown in Table 3.12.

Table 3.12: **Estimate of the number of injecting users with injecting site abscesses and infections**

	Not in Treatment	In treatment
Lowest estimate	37,483	No data
Medium estimate	44,980	
Highest estimate	67,470	

Other physical problems were chest pains. Other health issues associated with injecting are infective endocarditic, vein damage, lymphatic drainage, thrombosis, blood clots, and gangrene (BMA, 1997).

There is a lack of adequate information on these problems in the literature to enable assumptions to be made as to prevalence of the range of physical health problems associated with problem drug use.

All current injecting drug users risk HIV through sharing injecting paraphernalia, though the risk is reduced, in England and Wales, with low prevalence of HIV amongst the injecting community. Past injectors may already be infected with the disease; they also risk returning to injecting.

Estimates of prevalence are based on treatment samples and therefore we cannot extrapolate to problem users not in treatment. It is estimated that prevalence of HIV amongst injecting drug users is approximately two per cent in England and Wales (and Northern Ireland) (PHLS, 2001). Estimates based on both past and current injectors would yield 5,938 numbers of injecting users infected with HIV using the medium estimate of problem users.

A number of injecting drug users will be unaware that they are infected with HIV. PHLS suggests that a third of injecting drug users with HIV are unaware of their status. There are stages of HIV/AIDS; asymptomatic, symptomatic and AIDS. Information from PHLS suggests that of known HIV cases in the year 2000, 25.9 per cent were asymptomatic, 48.8 per cent were symptomatic, 28 per cent had AIDS and 1.8 per cent had died.

It is assumed, therefore, that amongst injecting users, 33 per cent are unaware (and probably asymptomatic, though not necessarily) leaving 66 per cent aware. This would yield an estimate of 1,799 HIV positive injectors being unaware of their status based on the medium estimate of problem users, 1,363 using the low estimate and 2,453 using the high estimate. This would therefore yield estimates of those with HIV being aware of their status as 2726, 3598 and 4907 using the low, medium or high estimate of the numbers in the problem drug using group respectively. The HIV status of those aware of their condition are shown in Table 3.13.

Table 3.13: HIV positive injectors HIV status

	Asymptomatic	Symptomatic	AIDS
Lowest estimate	706	1,330	736
Medium estimate	931	1,756	1,007
Highest estimate	1,270	2,395	1,373

Health-care costs vary at different stages of infection, and these have changed rapidly with changes in treatment and in particular the introduction of combination therapies. New treatments mean average annual costs of treating people with HIV are decreasing but lifetime costs are increasing. Previously the main costs associated with HIV/AIDS were following AIDS diagnosis and in particular inpatient care. It is now advised that treatment be offered soon after diagnosis (British HIV Association, 2001).

Expenditure estimates under combination therapy per person per year are:

- Asymptomatic   £13,381
- Symptomatic   £14,222
- AIDS   £24,314

Assuming all eligible patients are offered and take up treatment, the following costs are estimated, shown in Table 3.14. These costs do not include the costs of opportunistic infection associated with AIDS.

Table 3.14: Estimated annual costs of treatment for HIV infected drug users

	Asymptomatic	Symptomatic	AIDS	Total costs, £ million
Lowest estimate	£9,446,986	£18,915,260	£17,895,104	46.3
Medium estimate	£12,457,711	£24,973,832	£24,484,198	61.9
Highest estimate	£16,993,870	£34,061,690	£33,383,122	84.4

In addition some of these users will die each year. It is currently difficult to estimate how life expectancy may change with prolonged expectancy of asymptomatic and symptomatic HIV. The estimates in Table 4.14 are therefore shown as being indicative of the current order of magnitude of costs rather than being precise

The PHLS report prevalence of hepatitis B in injecting drug users, in 1999, as 25 per cent amongst those attending agencies in London and 17 per cent outside London. The combined estimate for England and Wales is approximately 21 per cent.

On the basis of these data the estimate of the numbers who are infected with Hepatitis are shown below.

Estimate of injecting drug users in England and Wales who have had or are currently infected with hepatitis B:
44,980 (lowest estimate)
53,975 (medium estimate)
80,964 (highest estimate)

NERA (2001) estimates the lifetime costs of treating patients with hepatitis and related conditions to be £4,300 per person. This assumes an average life expectancy of 30 additional years; an annual cost per person year of £143 per person per year. Given the estimated numbers this would suggest an annual treatment cost for hepatitis B in the order of £7.8 million.

The report to EMCDDA suggests the prevalence of hepatitis C infection among injecting drug users to be approximately 38 per cent in 1999 (UKADCU, 2000). PHLS reports that one-third of injecting drug users attending specialist agencies had antibodies to hepatitis C. Twenty per cent will develop chronic illnesses, including cirrhosis of the liver and the possibility of liver failure, though this can take several years.

Estimate of injecting drug users in England and Wales who have had or are currently infected with hepatitis C:

68,152 (lowest estimate)
81,782 (medium estimate)
122,673 (highest estimate)

If similar annual treatment costs to hepatitis B were assumed this would yield an annual cost of £11.7 million.

Infectious diseases relating to injecting drug use are likely to have a major impact on the social costs of drug use. Data to estimate these costs are limited and further research is required to determine the lifetime costs of these diseases. From the available data it is estimated that infectious diseases may be costing the health service some £80 million each year. However, some of these costs would have already been taken into account in the estimates of health-care expenditure among problem users, see Table 4.5 and this estimate is not used further in the main estimates of the social costs of Class A drug users.

Conclusions

The consequences of Class A drug use have been estimated for young recreational users, older regular users and problem drug users. No additional costs were calculated for either higher risk groups within the young recreational users or injecting drug users within the problem user group. For both these subgroups their consequences were seen to be included in the main estimates and no means or data were available to separate the consequences for these sub-groups from the rest of their group. Injecting drug use and the related health-care consequences are significant. The costs of caring for those infected will continue whether or not the individual leaves the drug-using population and that clearly has longer-term cost consequences.

Only health and crime consequences could be identified for young recreational users, see summary Table 3.15. The difference between reactive government expenditure and total social costs is wholly accounted for by the estimates for ecstasy-related deaths. This monetary estimate is a present value element related to the estimated year of death, but unlike other elements, could be thought to be borne across future years. The reactive government expenditure per young recreational users is calculated to be between £7.50 and £15. Total social costs are estimated to be between £36 and £72 per user.

Table 3.15: Estimated cost of consequences of young recreational users per year, £ million, 2000

Domain	Reactive government spending	Total social costs
Health	2.2	25.0
Work	No data	No data
Driving	No data	No data
Crime	3.8	3.8
Other Social	None identified	None identified
TOTAL	6.0	28.8

There is some evidence that there could be an impact of drug use on the productivity of young recreational users but there is no evidence of an impact on unemployment rates. The impact on productivity at work or educational achievement could be both long lasting and significant for this group even if the average impact was modest. There is also evidence of driving shortly after drug taking but there is no current means of estimating the likely risk of accidents from these data. Other potentially excluded impacts include: the impact of criminal convictions for possession on the individual's long-term career and employment; the concern about drug using among family members; impact of illicit markets for recreational users on the legitimate economy and the potential transmission risks to problem use.

For older regular users there was a similar pattern of government reactive costs. Crime costs, as for younger recreational users, are made up of criminal justice expenditure on drug arrests, see Table 3.16. With no deaths recorded for older regular users, government reactive costs and social costs are the same. The costs per user vary between £3 and £6. Driving impacts could be significant for the older regular user group as could productivity impacts. There are similar omitted consequences as for younger recreational users although some of the family concern about using could be assumed to lower.

Table 3.16: Estimated consequences for older regular users per year, £ million, 2000

	Reactive government expenditure	Total social cost
Health	2.4	2.4
Work	No data	No data
Driving	No data	No data
Crime	3.8	3.8
Other Social	None identified	None identified
TOTAL	6.2	6.2

The summary costs for problem drug users are shown in Table 3.17. Criminal justice costs are estimated to be the largest component of reactive government expenditure accounting for 67 per cent of the total, using the medium estimate. In terms of social consequences, victim costs of crime dominate at 88 per cent of the total, using the medium estimate. The reactive government expenditure per person is estimated at £10,402 and the total social cost at £35,455 per person using the medium estimate.

Table 3.17: Estimated consequences for problem drug users, £ million, 2000

Domain	Reactive government expenditure	Total social costs
Health – low	288	1,286
– medium	344	1,342
– high	514	1,512
Work – low	613	0
– medium	736	0
– high	1,094	0
Driving	No data	No data
Crime – low	1,972	8,797
– medium	2,366	10,556
– high	3,549	15,834
Other Social		
– low	53	53
– medium	63	63
– high	95	95
TOTAL – low	2,926	10,136
– medium	3,509	11,961
– high	5,252	17,441

Sensitivity analysis

The costs from problem users are dependent on the values given to different consequences and the split of this group among those in and out of treatment. The unit costs used were taken from a number of previously published sources. While a range of sensitivity analyses on these values could be undertaken it was outside the scope of this project. Rather some limited sensitivity analysis was conducted varying the numbers of problem drug users who were in and out of treatment, and the split of those in treatment between those in treatment more than or less than one year.

Increasing the assumed numbers in treatment from 33 per cent to 50 per cent would result in an estimated increase in reactive government expenditure of £5 million and decrease of social costs of £1,099 million. In contrast, assuming a lower proportion of problem drug users in treatment of 20 per cent, compared to the main estimate of 33 per cent, would result in an estimated decrease in government reactive expenditure of £4 million and an increase in social costs of £877 million. Changing the proportion of those in treatment for more than or less than one year from 50:50 to 80:20 or 20:80 would have the following results. If the proportion in treatment less than one year is 80 per cent, there would be an increase in reactive government expenditure of £90 million and a decrease in total social costs of £65 million compared to a 50:50 split. Reversing the proportion to 20 per cent in treatment less than one year would result in a decrease of government expenditure of £90 million and an increase in social costs of £65 million.

Combining the medium estimate of costs over all Class A drug users yields a total estimate annual reactive government expenditure of £3,251 million or £1,789 per user. Using the lowest estimates from the numbers of users and the sensitivity analysis would yield an estimate of £2,842 million. Using the highest estimates, including adding additional health costs for injecting drug users would yield an estimate of £5,439 million. The medium estimate of social costs is calculated as £11,996 million or £35,560 per user. The range of estimates is between £9,007 million and £18,523 million.

Assumption log

- Health costs and other social costs associated with ecstasy and other drug-related deaths are assumed to similar costs to those incurred by a road traffic accident death.
- Approximately half of those arrested for possession will be young people.
- Half of all cocaine use is recreational.
- Consequences for those in treatment differ from those not in treatment.
- Amongst problem users a third are currently in treatment, a third have previously been in treatment and a third have never been in treatment.
- Of those who have never been in treatment, two-thirds will be relatively young and may suffer fewer consequences as a result of drug use; though there is no literature evidence of how much less.
- A small but significant proportion of these may never enter treatment and will become drug-free without help; we assume a third. The remaining third of those who have never been in treatment we assume are extremely chaotic and suffer a disproportionately higher number of consequences.

- All our assumptions for those not in treatment are based on the same evidence; from drug users entering treatment, mainly drawn from the NTORS study.
- Of those assumed in treatment in any year, one half are assumed to have actively engaged or re-engaged in treatment in that year. Their consequences are assumed to be similar to those at one year after intake to the NTORS study.
- Of those assumed in treatment in any year, one half are assumed to have been actively engaged in treatment for over a year. Their consequences are assumed to be similar to those at two years after intake to the NTORS study.
- Actual criminal justice contacts from the NTORS study are taken to represent criminal justice costs, while victim costs of crime are based on self-reported offence data.

Research

The specific research needs are:

- The consequences of "recreational" use on productivity are not well understood.
- There is no evidence of the effect of drug use on driving.
- The nature of the causal relationship between problem drug use and mental health is not well researched.
- There are no data on the penalties imposed for possession of Class A recreational drugs.
- Little is understood about the consequences for problem drug users who have never been in treatment.
- More data are required linking consequences to treatment history
- Evidence of the treatment consequences for children, infectious disease and unemployment benefit is lacking.
- Further research is required to enable us to disentangle the consequences associated with injecting drug use and non-injecting drug use. There is strong evidence that non-injecting users are at risk of infections, such as hepatitis and even HIV though the extent of risk is not fully known.
- Generation of epidemiological evidence on health-related risks and how these risks vary with levels of use and across different types of use.
- To provide a more accurate public finance forecasting model in future work, additional research would be useful on the impact of changing activity on year-on-year health service and criminal justice systems. Other research is needed to determine a range of values for some of the major elements of such cross-government impacts and social issues such as the loss of drug users' lives.

4.   Summary and conclusions

Total economic costs or reactive expenditure is estimated to be £3.5 billion for Class A drug use in England and Wales, 2000 (medium estimate, range is £2.9bn to £5.3bn). This equates to some £1,927 averaged over all Class A drug users, and £10,402 averaged over problem drug users. The majority of the estimated costs are created by problem users.

Total social costs are substantially higher even though only limited data were available. The total estimate of consequences was £12 billion for 2000 (medium estimate, range is £10.1bn to £17.4bn). This equates to £6,564 per year averaged over all Class A drug users, £35,456 for problem drug users.

Discussion of key assumptions

In each chapter the many assumptions needed to make these calculations have been outlined. The main figures are the estimates of the different consequences by treatment status. These calculations are based upon available UK obtained data obtained from the NTORS study. This study has yielded comparable results to American treatment studies (Gossop *et al.*, 2001). The data from the period before the participants in NTORS entered the study were used to proxy for the costs of those problem users not in treatment. This is the key assumption for the estimates in the study. Any reduction in the costs of those not in treatment would imply there would be lower savings in either government reactive expenditure or total social costs for those in treatment from any estimates of the impact of changes in treatment numbers.

However, it could also be argued that using these estimates in any model underestimates the potential savings from treatment. First, some elements of the consequences of problem users were not available by treatment status, including impact on children and the unborn. Also, many of the longer-term impacts of treatment are not included, especially changes in infectious disease rates.

Estimates are also reliant on the impact of treatment and the time individuals are engaged with treatment services. The NTORS study shows problem drug users go in and out of addiction treatment. These effects are taken account of in the data used. However, at the time this study was undertaken, only two-year follow-up treatment data were available.

Differences in the estimates of the social costs impact were more substantial than those for reactive government expenditure. The estimates of those in treatment were just under a half of those out of treatment. It would be useful to have more empirical estimates to check the validity of the order of magnitude of these estimates.

Limitations of the proposed methodology and guidance for further research

The outline model provides a useful framework for estimation. The model's usefulness depends however on data availability. There is a lot of potential within the outline framework to undertake more specific modelling, particularly of longer-term impacts of drug use. This is an expanding field and a number of alternative mathematical and statistical approaches are available (Godfrey et al., 2001). As such models are developed there is scope for introducing more sophisticated modelling. The current schema has the advantage of being relatively simple in construction and the calculations can be replicated. More sophisticated models may be more realistic in the assumptions taken, but the computer calculations required would make it much harder to follow how the estimates have been constructed.

References

ACMD (2000) *Reducing drug related death.* A report by the Advisory Council on the misuse of Drugs. London: The Stationery Office.

Anderson, S. and Frischer, M. (1997) *Recreational Drugs and Driving.* Drugs Misuse in Scotland.

Boreham, R. and Shaw, A. (2001) *Smoking, drinking and drug use among young people in England in 2000.* London: The Stationery Office.

Brand, S. and Price, R (2000) *The economic and social costs of crime.* Home Office Research Study 217 Economic and Resource Analysis, Research, Development and Statistics Directorate. London: Home Office.

British HIV Association (2001) *British HIV Association (BHIVA) guidelines for the treatment of HIV-infected adults with antiretroviral therapy.* London: BHIVA.

British Medical Association (1997) The Misuse of Drugs. Netherlands: Harwood.

Buck, D., Godfrey, C. and Sutton, M. (1996) Economic and other views of addiction: implications for the choice of alcohol, tobacco and drug policies, *Drug and Alcohol Review*, 15: 357-368.

Coid, J., Carvell, A., Kittler, Z., Healey, A. and Henderson, J. (2000) *Opiates, criminal behaviour and methadone treatment.* Home Office Research Findings 120 London: Home Office www.homeoffice.gov.uk/rds/pdfs/crimbehav.pdf.

Corkery, J.M. (2001) *Drug seizures and offender statistics, United Kingdom, 1999.* London: Home Office.

Culyer, A., Eaton, G., Godfrey, C., Koutsolioutsos, H., and McDougall, C. (2002) *Economic & Social Cost of Substance Misuse in the United Kingdom: Review of the methodological and empirical studies of the economic and social costs of illicit drugs.* Report to the Home Office: University of York.

Department of the Environment, Transport and the Regions (1999) *Road accidents in Great Britain: 1988 the Casualty Report.* London: DETR.

Department of Health (2001a) *Statistics from the Regional Drug Misuse Databases for six months ending September 2000.* London: Department of Health.

Department of Health (2001b) *Hospital Episode Statistics. 2000.* London: Department of Health, www.doh.gov.uk/hes

Department of Local Government, Transport and the Regions (2001) Road Accidents in Great Britain: 1998 the Casualty Report. London: DTLR, www.roads,dtlr.gov.uk/roadsafety/hen2000/05.htm

Eaton, G. (1998) An Evaluation of a Pilot Project to Develop an Integrated Model of Shared Care. Liverpool Health Authority.

EMCDDA (1997) Estimating the scale and nature of drug problems: the relationship between science, policy and drugs strategy. In *Estimating the prevalence of problem drug use in Europe.* European Monitoring Centre for Drugs and Drug Addiction Scientific Monograph No. 1, Luxembourg: Office for Official Publications of the European Communities.

Emmerson, C. and Lancaster, A. (2000) *A Survey of the UK Benefit System.* Institute of Fiscal Studies Briefing notes No. 13 www.ifs.org.uk/taxsystem/benefitsurvey

Frischer, M., Hickman, M., Kraus, L, Mariani, F. and Wiessing, L. (2001) A comparison of different methods for estimating problematic drug misuse in Great Britain. *Addiction* 96:1465-1476.

Ghodse, H., Oyefeso, O., Hunt, M., Pollard, M., Webb, L., Corkery, J (2001) *Drug-related Deaths reported by Coroners in England & Wales January to June, 2000.* np-SAD Surveillance Report No.6 National Programme on Substance Abuse Deaths, 2001 London: St George's Hospital.

Goddard, E and Higgins, V. (1999) *Smoking, drinking and drug use among young teenagers in 1998.* London: The Stationery Office.

Godfrey, C. and Maynard, A. (1995) Economic Evaluation of alcohol policies. In Edwards, G. and Holder, H. (eds) *The Scientific Rationale for Alcohol Policy.* Oxford: Oxford University Press.

Godfrey, C., Stewart, S. and Gossop, M. (2002) *National Treatment Outcome Research Study: Economic Analysis of the Two Year Outcome Data.* Report to the Department of Health.

Godfrey, C., Wiessing, L. and Hartnoll, R. (scientific eds.) (2001) *Modelling drug use: methods to quantify and understand hidden processes.* EMCDDA Monograph No 6. Lisbon: EMCDDA.

Gossop, M., Marsden, J., Stewart, D., Edwards, C., Lehmann, P., Wilson, A., and Segar, G. (1996) *The National Treatment Outcome Research Study: Summary of the project, the clients and preliminary findings: First Bulletin.* London: Department of Health.

Gossop, M., Marsden, J., and Stewart, D. (1998) *NTORS at one year: changes in substance use, health and criminal behaviour one year after intake.* London: Department of Health.

Gossop, M., Marsden, J. and Steward, D. (2001) *NTORS After Five Years: Changes in substance use, health and criminal behaviour during the five years after intake.* London: National Addiction Centre.

Goulden, C. and Sondhi, A. (2001) *At the margins: drug use by vulnerable young people: results from the 1998/9 Youth Lifestyle Survey.* Home Office Research Study No. 228. London: Home Office.

Harries, R. (1999) *The costs of criminal justice.* Home Office Research, Development and Statistics Directorate, Research Findings 103, London: Home Office.

Ingram, D., Lancaster, B. and Hope, S. (2001) *Recreational Drugs and Driving: Prevalence Survey.* System Three Research. The Scottish Executive Central Research Unit 200. www//scotland.gov.uk/cru/kdo.1/blue/prevalence-06.htm

National Statistics (2001) *Mid-2000 population estimates.* London: Office of National Statistics.

NERA (2001) *Estimating the Cost of Drug Misuse to the NHS.* Report to the Department of Health, unpublished.

Netten, A. and Curtis, L (2000) *Unit Costs of Health and Social Care.* Canterbury: PSSRU, University Of Kent.

NHS Schedule of Reference Costs (2000) London: Department of Health National Statistics/Department of Health (2001) *Children looked after in England. 1999/2001.* London: Department of Health.

National Programme on Substance Abuse Deaths. London: St George's Hospital PHLS (2001) *AIDS/HIV Cumulative Data to End June 2001*. Report No. 51: 01/2 London: Department of Health.

Pollard, M. (2001) Personal communication on ecstasy deaths for 2000.

Ramsey, M., Baker, P., Goulden, C., Sharp, C. and Sondhi, A. (2001) *Drug misuse declared in 2000: results from the British Crime Survey*. Home Office Research Study 224 London: Home Office (raw data).

Sondhi A. (2001) personal communication. Home Office.

Stewart, D (2001) personal communication. National Treatment Outcome Research Study. National Addiction Centre. Institute of Psychiatry.

UKADCU (2000) *UK Drug Situation 2000: The UK report to the European Monitoring Centre for Drugs and Drug Addiction*. London: The Cabinet Office.

RDS Publications

Requests for Publications

Copies of our publications and a list of those currently available may be obtained from:

Home Office
Research, Development and Statistics Directorate
Communication Development Unit
Room 275, Home Office
50 Queen Anne's Gate
London SW1H 9AT
Telephone: 020 7273 2084 (answerphone outside of office hours)
Facsimile: 020 7222 0211
E-mail: publications.rds@homeoffice.gsi.gov.uk

alternatively

why not visit the RDS website at
           Internet: http://www.homeoffice.gov.uk/rds/index.html

where many of our publications are available to be read on screen or downloaded for printing.

Standai
The College, Merthyr Tv
Tel: 0168⁵

ᵤₒ Best Paddle Sport Games

Fourth Edition 2005

Loel Collins
Author and Technical Editor for this edition.

Dave Ruse
Author and Editor of the previous editions.

Peter Knowles
General Editor

Rivers Publishing UK

Photographs are as credited.

Design by www.matrix1solution.co.uk
Cover design by Leon Reichel.

Drawings are by Dave Ruse. Cartoons are by Alan Fox (Foxy).
First published 1986, A & C Black Ltd,
Second edition 1994, A & C Black Ltd
Third edition 2000, Rivers Publishing U.K.
Fourth edition 2005, Rivers Publishing U.K.

ISBN: 0-9550614-0-7

A CIP catalogue record for this book is available from the British
Library.

Printed by Cambrian Printers in Wales. www.cambrian-printers.co.uk

Trade enquiries:

- **U.K. and Europe:** to Cordee Outdoor Books & Maps,
  3a De Montford St, Leicester LE1 7HD, UK.
  www.cordee.co.uk   Fax: 0116 247 1176.
- **North America** to Alpen Books,
  4602 Chennault Beach Rd, Ste B1, Mukiteo, WA 98275, USA.
  www.alpenbooks.com   Fax: 425 493 6381
- **Other countries:** to Rivers Publishing U.K.
  Gower, Blencathra St, Keswick, CA12 4HW, UK.
  www.riverspublishing.co.uk

Disclaimer
All canoe and kayak games can be dangerous - they rely on the
coach or person running the game to avoid injury or worse. If you
decide to play one of these games, the risk assessment is yours, the
decision to play the game is yours, and the consequences arising
from that decision are yours and yours alone. The publishers, editors
and contributors can accept no responsibility for any loss or injury
sustained by any person as a result of ideas expressed in this book.

Foreword

Well, I m a very proud and humbled guy in that twenty years after I first wrote it, Canoe Games is still selling well and I am delighted that it has now being brought up to date with this new colourful and exciting edition.

I think I first got the idea for a games leaflet when I was teaching a BCU Senior Instructors course at the Adur Centre at Shoreham on Sea - I did most of my teaching by using games - both to improve the skills like balance, but also to develop the things you don t see in the manuals, like team work. My pupils must have thought, here we go again, guinea pigs for Rusey, but they all really liked the games and they progressed fast.

A few years later I gave a lecture at Plas y Brenin about teaching canoeing in the city and how successful canoe games were at capturing the interest of street wise kids. The staff at Plas y Brenin were really encouraging and said Dave, you should write a book? - so of course I did! It was Plas y Brenin that nurtured the original book, and now twenty years later I am really pleased that they have helped produce this brand new edition for the 21st Century.

I still have lots of photos and fond memories of compiling the first edition, which was mainly based on my work with city kids in central London. Canoe Games proved surprisingly popular and it is nice to know that the book has been used all over the world in all kinds of exotic countries.

One of the nicest things about writing a book is that wherever you go, you meet your readers. I live in Cornwall now and help crew the local lifebot, and at the end of one rescue operation I was chatting to the Coastguard Officer who said I don t suppose you d be Dave Ruse of Canoe Games? So the book brought me a litlle fame, and it also encouraged me to write another book called City Adventures about ideas for working with City kids, (for which I won a Sir Winston Churchill Scholarship). This again was quite successful and was translated into German.

So well done to everyone who has helped put this new edition together!

Now, less chat - go out and try some of these games!

Dave Ruse (last seen surfing a wave in Cornwall)

Lou Manouch

Contents

Introduction

When I started training as a coach, some twenty years ago, Dave Ruse s book was at the top of my useful reading list. With the enthusiasm of a puppy I got hold of the book and tried out almost everything in it. I found my favourites and my dislikes. I found the good games that seemed to do particular jobs and I started creating my own. The book got lost over the years but the games stuck with me, sometimes tuned or renamed as fashions changed. It s only on re-reading this book that I realise how many of the games I d almost thought of as my own were in those pages and it just serves to confirm that original thought is a rare commodity!

This book isn t one person s work and we would like to say a really big thank you to all the contributors for the games they sent in. We received over 300 games and reviewed them all. We grouped similar games and then created sub-groups of duplicate games. We then looked at each group for games we recognised and those we didn t and then we tried out the games we didn t know or that just seemed like good fun! The whole process did two things; It served to echo the last statement above, however it also served to show the ingenuity and resourcefulness of the coaches who contributed.

We hope you will find your favourite game in this book, unfortunately it may be under someone else s name as we had problems with several games knowing who to credit they haven t stolen your thunder they ve complimented you! It s the sincerest form of flattery! Importantly, it is the nature and strength of the way we all teach, by sharing. It was very difficult to choose to include or omit games from the huge number we received. I have to admit the easiest was the dead fish canoe polo! However, nothing else was!

Some games may seem fun, some stupid, and some just impossible - find out for yourself. We did just this we tried out these games with our centre assistants, unsuspecting coaches on coach education courses, and with kids and adults on various sessions. I would like to say a big thank you to these knowing, and not so knowing, guinea pigs!

Good paddling!

Loel Collins,

Head of Canoeing,
Plas y Brenin National Mountaineering Centre. U.K.
www.pyb.co.uk

Why Play Games ?

Is it just me - or have we become so bound up in the specifics and details of what and how we teach that we ve lost that intangible stuff that actually made things fun? I think that maybe we have.

We ve ended up hiding behind the pseudo science of teaching, games have become periods of practice, trying it on both sides is now called bi-lateral practice, ENOUGH!! Good teaching is an art - it has to be an art because it s about changing how people feel - just like music, poetry and photography. We know that if we feel happy we learn more, we become confident and feel better in ourselves, indeed we are less likely to become ill or to injure ourselves. PLAYING GAMES MAKES THINGS FUN!

As a professional coach I use games, sometimes disguised as exercises, or hidden by a thin veneer of adult seriousness because they work. You can find a game that works well in almost any water situation or weather condition. The venue may be a city, open lake, the sea, white water river, or even indoors in the small, confined area of a swimming pool. It is even possible to play some canoe games without any water!

The main point is that games are fun and people enjoy them. Paddlers loosen up, stop worrying about how silly they might look or how wet they may get. Many games can be used either during a particular session or to make a specific location more interesting. They give all paddlers confidence in their relationship with their equipment and in the environment.

It s a human characteristic that as we become successful at something our confidence grows and as our confidence grows it helps us go beyond that original area of success. Games develop confidence because a successful game is simply fun.

Safety

Games are for fun. However fun must never overshadow the safety of the players. Canoeing and kayaking are physical sports, and from time to time people may get hurt and equipment damaged. It is therefore essential to have a first aid kit to hand and be able to recognise the potential for injury or accident as and when it develops.

It is possible to cut down on the number of accidents by keeping a watchful eye on how the game is progressing and sticking to the following guidelines. These guidelines are based on experience and on an ongoing risk assessment process throughout the game and session. It is essential to assess the risk of a particular game, with a particular group, and in the particular conditions that day. What is safe with one group on a particular day may not be on another day with a different group. For these reason these are guidelines NOT laws — and these go hand in hand with your experience NOT replacing it!

Some helpful advice:

1. Firstly be qualified and/or competent to run the activity.

2. Ensure the equipment in use is safe, serviceable, properly maintained and appropriate for use by the group (size, fittings, etc.)

3. Make sure the group have a **safety briefing** before any particular game, and for example know what to do if someone capsizes and what is the signal if you need to STOP the session (people can easily get carried away when playing games).

4. Plan beforehand and consider your game within the whole session — for example the group may need to be prepared for the game with particular skills.

5. When you have selected a game consider the hazards and follow normal practice to manage the risks, e.g. Tag is a physical game, people can be hit with a paddle, so it would be sensible and good practice to wear helmets.

6. Your club or centre should have a written risk assessment that covers paddling activities as a whole. On any particular day, it is your decision as a coach whether to run a game and you should be thinking is this safe and appropriate for this group in these particular circumstances? This is what we call a dynamic risk assessment and obviously in most circumstances it would be impractical to have this written down!

7. Keep reminding yourself - Having fun must not be at the expense of safety!

Boats

You can use kayaks, canoes, sit on tops and even duckies for games. Many of these boats are made of tough plastic with few fitting that could break or go wrong. Games are tough on boats so some thought should be given to ensuring the craft is game toughened .

1. The boats and equipment should be checked prior to the session and anything sub-standard removed to prevent it being used.

2. Buoyancy and airbags should be fitted and secured.

3. Seats should be secured.

4. Thick handles or toggles should be fitted as end grabs for kayaks, canoes need only have a short bow painter. Sit on tops will not need straps for most games.

5. Rounded ends are best, to protect other people and boats.

6. Smooth rounded gunnels are best on canoes as people run along them with their hands, arms and legs.

7. Kayaks should have large cockpits. These are better for getting in and out.

Plas y Brenin   *Safety Briefing*

9

Equipment

Balls

Many games involve the throwing and catching of balls. Solid, heavy or overly inflated balls all have the potential to injure and hurt. Not only that, football sized balls can easily trap exit from a kayak if placed within the cockpit. Light balls are hard when wet. Sponge balls can become too heavy to throw. Very large balls can be great fun but are impossible to pick up or carry on a boat, and a nightmare if it s windy!

The moral of the story is **pick your ball carefully!**

Balloons

Balloons are great - they take a bit of time to inflate and are fun to burst! Just make sure you clean up the debris!

Buoys and Weights

These are really useful to mark out areas and to create definite boundaries or start and finish points. Use a buoy, and a length of rope weighted with a short length of chain. The buoys needn t be heavily weighted - that way they can be moved around the lake as required and taken in at the end of the day.

Hoops

Hula hoops have endless uses, brightly coloured plastic ones are ideal. They can float or be hung up (for example from a branch) as goals.

Clothes Pegs

A bag of giant, brightly coloured plastic clothes pegs can be useful for some Tag games, but note that they often don t float - see below for alternatives.

Plas y Brenin

Pipe Lagging

This is great stuff to have around, in long lengths, short lengths, and preferably different colours. You will get through a lot of it. It will need clearing up afterwards! Short lengths in different colours can be used like pegs to clip onto end grabs, and identify teams.

Sponges

These are easily carried and can be used instead of balls (a horrid, nasty, wet idea) or used instead of clothes pegs jammed under end grabs, to identify different teams, or for tag games (different colours are best). They can even be used to empty out water.

Blind Folds

Blindfolds can add a whole new dimension to many games, but should be chosen with care as they could cause panic in a capsize. Choose ones that can be removed easily.

Mouse Tails

Small lengths of floating rope can be used in tag games and are easy to find at the end of a session.

A Plank (for walking)

Free of splinters and secured with rope or bungy.

Rope

Floating rope is best, brightly coloured and around 8mm thick. A million uses. Always have a knife handy!

Yellow Plastic DUCKS

Be kind to your web-footed friends. These are great props - to herd, find, chase carry, and generally have fun - just like bath time!

WHISTLE or fog horn

For group control and to STOP the game.

Lou Manouch

How To Use This Book

The games in this book have many uses and are suitable for a variety of situations and conditions. This is essentially a reference and ideas book for dipping into in order to select a few games for the day, your group, and situation.

To help in that process we have done our best to group games together logically, a difficult task because many games could happily fit in several different chapters. Also check out the **lists of games** in Appendix A.

At the start of each chapter you will find a summary table -

Game

We have numbered all the games for easy reference. We have left some blank numbers at the end of each section so you can add your own games.

Boat

What type of boat this game is probably suitable for - **K**= Kayak, **C** = Open Canoe, **S** = Sit on top.

Wetness Rating

This is the likelihood of the participants getting wet and is obviously a vital factor when choosing a game (do you really want your group to get wet, cold and miserable?). We have used colour coding -

Dry	=	dry land game
Damp	=	afloat but should stay reasonably dry.
Wet	=	some chance of splashing and accidental capsize.
Swim	=	a high probability of a swim or similar.

Level

Is the suggested level/s that the game is suitable for - linked to the British Canoe Union 1 to 5 star tests.

(As a rough guide - 1 is a beginner, 5 is an expert).

Skill development

Canoe and Kayak games can help a person develop many attributes and skills, not just simply paddle waggling! We have tried to highlight some of these skills in the table at the start of the chapter. For a young person many of these coordination and movement skills are important in terms of long term development. Many games improve understanding of basic things like action and reaction, push and pull, balance and imbalance - these are important for young people, but games can also help the older paddler revise, and in some cases rethink the basics.

www.focussed-on-adventure.com

Learning through playing games does not necessarily happen by right: the coach needs to highlight particular aspects of a skill and choose a game that is appropriate for that skill development to ensure the game is beneficial for the participants. Playing games is a fantastic way of providing challenges and opportunities for paddlers to develop skills, but they need to be carefully chosen to ensure they achieve the desired outcome and help the coach reach their goals for the session.

Strokes
The majority of the games in this book use many different paddle strokes, but where we think a game helps practice or develop one or two specific paddle strokes we have highlighted this in the summary table and alongside the games description.

Good
This is our subjective paddle rating. We took into account things like:
- how easy a game was to set up and run,
- what resources were needed,
- was the game easy for the group to understand?
- does the game develop useful skills?
- is the game fun and popular?

If you don't agree with our rating, then write your own in the margin!

Add your own game
We have tried to design this book so that there is plenty of space so you can add your own games and notes. If you think that you have a really different and innovative game then why not share it with others? Send it to the BCU Code magazine, or send it to us and we will try and include it on our website www.riverspublishing.co.uk.

Acknowledgements

Many thanks to all the coaches and paddlers who contributed and helped produce this edition - without your help, this book would not have been possible:

Marcus Bailie
Geoff Barrett
Martin Barry
Chris Bate
Liz Beard
Dave Bennett
Mathew Bishop
Andy Boothman
Mark Brian
Norman Brooks
Dave Brown
Paul Burgess
Glynn Carter
Helen Carter
Pete Catteral
Lawrence Chapman
Melhonie Cheseldine
Martin Chester
Grant Cockerill
Mark Corps
Andy Craven
Ruth Craven
Rosie Diver
James Donnell
Chas Donnelly
Carwyn Dwyer
Bob Evans
Glyn Evans-Hughes
Tim Freeman
Caroline Gerritsen
Richard Gill

Emma Goodall
Barry Gray
John Spike Green
Phil Hadley
Simon Hammond
Dave Hart
Martyn Hartley
Kev Hawkes
Sue Hawthorn
Mike Heslop
Leo Hoare
Ruth Holdway
Suzy Hornby
Paul Hurrell
Martin Hurrell
Tom Laws
Dave Luke
Phil Lyon
Greer Mackenzie
Nicky Marsh
Lester Mathews
Karl Midlane
Stuart Miller
Jeremy Morland
Dicky Mott
Mark Nichols
Suresh Paul
Rosemary Powell
Dave Rosseter
Paul Steadman

Allan Shaw
Les Stewart
Charlie Stretton
Norman Teasdale
Helen Teasdale
Peter Terry
Bob Timms
Lara Tipper
David Tolfree
Bob Walker
Mark Walker
Graham Watson
Dave Williams
Kath Wright

PHOTOGRAPHS
Karl Midlane
Lou Manouch
Outdoor Adventure
Plas y Brenin
Peter Knowles
PGL Travel
Pesda Press
Dave Leathborough
Sue Ottoline
Lester Mathews
Rob White
Shoreline Activities
Leicester Outdoor
Pursuits Centre

WARM UP GAMES (Dry Land)

The advantage of doing a warm up is that it sets the tone for your session and it enables you as a coach to communicate and empathise with group. It s good practice and goes someway to reducing the possibility of injuries in the session due to over exertion - sports scientists tell us that our bodies work best when they are warmer.

Almost any physical activity can be used to help warm up so long as the progression is gentle and graduated. Gradually increasing the intensity of activity at the start of your session is a good thing to build in but sometimes this isn t practical because boats have to be moved around etc. - so a warm up game is then a great idea.

At the end of the session warming down is also important. It s often over looked! Simply reducing the intensity of activity in your session will go a long way, however a better idea may be to end with a cohesive game that leaves everyone feeling good. Using a warming down game is a great way to end the session, and should help alleviate the effects of exertion during the session, reducing muscle soreness and improving flexibility in the long term.

Lots of fun games can be developed with a bit of imagination, but you will need to be quite up front and out-going for this! These are all dry land games — this keeps things under control, and ensures that it is a warm up, rather than a cool down!

Game	Boat	Skill Development.	Level	Stroke		Good?
1. Scissors, Paper, Stone	---	Short and long term flexibility, rotation, active posture, balance, awareness, core stability, dodging, co-ordination, vision, agility and acceleration.	All	N/A		▌▌
2. Endless knot	---	As above	All	N/A	Dry	▌
3. Journey to the moon	---	As above	All	N/A	Dry	▌▌
4. Supermarket sweep	---	As above	All	N/A	Dry	▌▌
5. The Derby	---	As above	All	N/A	Dry	▌▌
6. Paddle Swap	---	As above	All	N/A	Dry	▌▌
7. Trip to the Zoo	---	As above	All	N/A	Dry	▌▌
8. Paddle Spin	---	As above	All	N/A	Dry	▌▌
9. Paddle twist	---	As above	All	N/A	Dry	▌▌
10. Run Around	---	As above	All	N/A	Dry	▌▌
11. Paddle swoop	---	As above	All	N/A	Dry	▌▌
12. Sticky Paddles	---	As above	All	N/A	Dry	▌▌
13. Paddle Yoga	---	As above	All	N/A	Dry	▌▌
14. Beans	---	As above	All	N/A	Dry	▌▌▌
15. Let s Dance	---	As above	All	N/A	Dry	▌▌▌
16. Rapids	---	As above	All	N/A	Dry	▌
17. Boat Gym	K	As above	All	N/A	Dry	▌▌
18. Paddle walk	---	As above + Team work	All	N/A	Dry	▌▌
19. Tarp Games	---	As above	All	N/A	Dry	▌
20. Rope Tricks	---	As above	All	N/A	Dry	▌
21. Canoe Twister	C	As above + knowledge of boats	All	N/A	Dry	▌▌▌

DRY = Dry Land Game

DAMP = Afloat but should stay dry

WET = Some chance of splashing and accidental capsize

SWIM = High probability of a swim or similar

... how we would have evolved if paddles hadn't been invented...

1 Scissors, Paper, Stone

You will need one paddle and two helmets for this game (or some similar markers). Take your players and divide into two teams, each team stands opposite each other using the paddle on the ground as the centre line. Show them the traditional game of scissors, paper and stone on hands and then transfer this to the whole body

- For scissors - do a star jump shape,
- For paper - a long tall stretch,
- For stone - crouch right down into a tuck.

Place each helmet 10-15m away from the paddle centre-line behind each team. Each team now jogs off to the pre-placed helmets and then decide as a team whether to do scissors, paper or stone. The team then jogs back to the centre-line / paddle, where, on the count of 3 by the coach, the teams battle it out. A trial run may be required! Continue until a team gets to 3 or 5 wins, or until suitably warmed up. Note that inevitably there may be score draws, i.e. rock against rock.

More energetic variation: the team that makes the winning shape, i.e. paper against stone, has to chase the losing team back to their safe place (the helmet). If any of the losing team members are tagged before reaching the helmet they then join the winning team.

Ruth Craven and Dave Brown

Peter Knowles

2 Endless knot
Level 1-5

Have your group stand in a large circle, holding hands to form a loop. Pick a person at random and get them to go under the arms of two of the people next to them, and then the chain of people follow - this creates an endless knot.
Martin Grinner Hurrell

3 Journey to the moon
Level 1-5

We are going for a journey to the moon, What do we need? A rocket! Draw a rocket in the air with your finger, don t forget the door and the handle, open the door and get in, stay standing, flick all the switches, handbrake off, arms ready on the throttle, count down from 10, when you get to 5 every one starts jogging and the countdown continues the pace increases until you reach take off and you all push the throttle forwards, keep running on the spot to get out of orbit , once you ve broken out of the atmosphere you can throttle back and start floating around with big exaggerated actions picking up and putting on your paddling kit as if your putting a space suit in preparation for landing on the moon. So everyone has to get back into position ready to land. As the gravity increases you have to start throttling up to fight the gravity until you land, Now the groups has landed you have to get out onto the lunar surface and go and collect your lunar exploration equipment (paddle and boats) all of this has to be done in zero gravity so all the movements have to be large, slow and careful.
Loel Collins

4 Supermarket sweep
Level 1-5

The group pretend to follow you around the supermarket. Each pretends to push a trolley. They have to reach for items on the top shelf and get low for ones on the bottom shelf. You could pretend that you forgot something on an aisle and have to go back for it.
Lawrence Chapman

5 The Derby
Level 1-5

Each pretends to be a jockey in the stalls, the race is off including jumps, corners, water jumps, etc.
Lawrence Chapman

6 Paddle Swap
Level 1-5

For this game, have your group standing in a circle equally spaced, with their paddles held up vertically in one hand, at arms length, with one blade on the ground in front of them. If you give the command 'Left' the people in the group will let go of their paddles and step left to where the person to the left of them was and at the same time grab that person s paddle before it drops to the ground. Likewise if the command 'Right' is given, the group will do the opposite. When people become too good, then speed up the commands, or two paddles to the right , etc.

Geoff Barrett

Lou Manouch

7 Trip to the Zoo
Level 1-5

Each member of the group is a penguin trying to escape from the zoo. First of all they have to hide from the zoo keeper, run for cover to their own enclosure and dive and swim across their pool to get away from the zoo keeper. They jump from the water only to discover that they have landed in the polar bear s pen so they then have to impersonate a polar bear to avoid being eaten or caught. The impersonation doesn t work so they have to run fast to the next enclosure which belongs to the gorillas so now they have to sit down with the gorillas and pretend to eat bananas but their penguin wings don t allow them to do this so they get sussed and have to run away again, this time by jumping the high fence. You can have the group run and hide in as many different enclosures as you like favourites of mine are the orang-utans who swing through the trees to escape, and the elephants who have to reach forwards with their trunks to steal buns from the visitors - and of course you will now be getting hungry after all this running around!

Loel Collins

8 Paddle Spin   Level 1-5

For this game, you will have to split the group into 2 equal teams, (this works best if you either have a larger ratio, or have 2 separate groups). The teams will stand one behind the other at a 'start line' then about 10 or so metres away will be 2 paddles (one for each team). When you say 'go', the first person in each team will then run up to their paddle, lift the paddle up and hold the paddle vertically (straight up and down) with the bottom blade against their chest. Once they have hold of the paddle they then have to do 10 complete spins on the spot as fast as they can. Once they have done the spins, they then put the paddle down and run back (if they can as they will be dizzy) to the next person in their team who will then go. First team back will be the winners. If you want to make this a bit more interesting have the teams run to the paddles forwards, do the spins, then run back backwards. (N:B. this game should only be played on grass or sand).   *Geoff Barratt*

9 Paddle twist   Level 1-5

Stand back to back with a partner with both hands on the paddle shaft. With the paddle held vertically rotate around and pass it to your partner. Repeat ten times. In the same starting position pass the paddle over your head for your partner to collect and pass it back between your legs.

Paul Hurrell

Peter Knowles

10 Run Around

Level 1-5

Space the groups equipment out over a reasonable area so that people will not run into each other. On the count of three, everyone runs and touches the front of every kayak/ canoe and then returns, this is repeated for stern, cockpit, sit in each boat, etc. Set the boats out as a series of hurdles to jump, put the paddle on the ground to do hops round, use the helmets to make a slalom course.

11 Paddle swoop

Level 1-5

BEACH

Stand in a large circle with a paddle each, lay the paddle down so the blade is by your feet and write your initials in the sand under your blade. Run around the outside of the paddle circle until you return to your paddle (repeat varying the direction, type of travel etc. For example touch the first blade and do a star jump by the second etc. In-between each run you can do a stretch)   *Paul Hurrell*

12 Sticky Paddles

Level 1-5

With a partner, stand on a line standing one behind the other with one paddle between the pair. Number 1 runs 30m to another line carrying the paddle and returns to pass it to their partner who does the same. Repeat varying the method of travel. For example: - both holding the paddle one running backwards and one running forwards, Hands on your head with the paddle gripped between you and your partners thighs (like a hobby horse race), get the paddle to the other line without moving whilst holding the paddle (pass and run, like netball) etc.

Paul Hurrell

13 Paddle Yoga

Level 1-5

This is another favourite warm up or lunchtime pastime. Paddle-passing around the body is a test of suppleness. Each player has a paddle and holds this out in front of them. They are not allowed to move or release their hands from the paddles. The sort of things they can try are: stepping over the paddle; passing it around their back and over their head to where they started. Try it and see; there are some very complicated moves that can be worked out.

Peter Knowles

14 Beans
Level 1-5

The theme of this warm up is Beans, surprise, surprise! The coach has to demonstrate as well! The First Beans are **runner beans**- the group runs on the spot, they need to do this for a short while, once running the coach shouts **broad beans** and adopts a sumo wrestling type position and then returns to runner beans. After a short while the coach now shouts **jumping beans**, the group jump! Then back to broad beans and then runner beans. From then on let your imagination run with it. Try Mexican beans, baked beans, has beans, string beans and what about Mr Beans or recently beans.
Suresh Paul

15 Let s Dance
Level 1-5

Similar, in structure to Beans - but great for Tandem canoe crews, This time your crews pair up to dance, they can waltz, can-can, pogo, salsa, disco, jive, twist.
Leo Hoare

16 Rapids
Level 1-5

This game needs space, and although on dry land it has the advantage of practicing paddling skills. Everyone has a paddle and paddle and run (walk) around in a follow my leader type of game - turn corners, stops, paddle backwards etc. Try running a rapid - break in, surf & wave, etc
Lawrence Chapman

17 Boat Gym
Level 1-5

Use your kayak rather like a gymnastic box. Run around it, complete bench jumps from one side to the other. Try bunny jumps with your hands on the back of the boat and jumping the legs from one side to the other.
Paul Hurrell

Peter Knowles

22

18 Paddle walk
Level 1-5

This is a slightly similar game to the 16 above, except paddlers are in teams of four, and imagine that they are in a K4 kayak. Each paddler stands one behind the other but slightly offset so that the back person can still see the front person. The leader goes through a variety of paddle strokes and builds up the speed and intensity as the crew try to walk forwards but keeping the paddling in time. Try this as a Dragon boat, or a C8 .

Paul Hurrell

19 Tarp Games
Level 1-5

TARP & BALL

Have your group all stand around the outside edge of your tarp (emergency group shelter), holding the edge with both hands. You ll need a large clear area for this! The group have to keep hold, and start walking clock-wise or anti-clock wise, allow the pace to quicken, on the shout low the group, whilst still moving, have to bend their legs so the tarp is as close to the ground as they can get it. On the command High the group have to reach for the sky. Keep jogging round, but this time shout switch so the team change direction. You could also try jump, Hop , and Skip . With practice you could have the group reach high so the tarp billow up high enough to run to the middle and out again.

If you have two or three small tarps you could try having one group reach high to form an arch with the tarp as the other group run underneath, to then form another arch for the next team to run under.

Another game is to place a large ball in the tarp, The idea is to try and get the ball to do laps of the tarp by co-ordinating the raising and lowering of the tarp. Another variation is to try throwing the ball up off the tarp and then catching it again..

Loel Collins

20 Rope Tricks
Level 1-5

Peter Knowles

THROW ROPE

Empty your throw line/tracking lines onto the floor. Pair your group and then they each take an end of the rope. On the word go the rope is pulled in hand over hand until it becomes tight and the other person is pulled forwards.

Loel Collins

This requires a little bit of preparation, You ll need to make two spinning dials, a laminated piece of card with a dial in the middle will do. One of the cards is split into quarters, each quarter will have either left foot, right foot, left hand, right hand written in it. The dial can be spun to point into either quarter at random. The second is split into eights, each with a part of the boat written into it, the dial can be spun to point, randomly to any part of the boat. First spin the body dial to select a part of the body, then spin the boat dial to select a part of the boat. The paddler has to do what the dial says. Next go, the dials are spun again, the next body part has to go to the next boat part without loosing contact of the first.

Loel Collins

Why? when it has taken so long to get changed and warmed up.....

do you suddenly get desperate for a pooh?

Enjoy the experience of their lifetime.

If there's one thing we pride ourselves on at Plas y Brenin, it's our staff. Our coaches are amongst the most experienced, highly qualified and enthusiastic in the country. Not only can we boast as many as 13 Level 5 coaches along with a further 9 Level 5 aspirants, but our coaching team also includes national coaches, several former national squad members, nationally recognised experts in safety and rescue, numerous authors, and expert advisors to a wide range of governing bodies.

Putting aside their professional experience, our coaches have amassed an unrivalled compendium of international expeditions, ground-breaking solo navigations and first descents spanning every continent. All of which goes to enrich their coaching skills and leads to a more interesting, rewarding and inspiring learning-experience for you.

But the final and most important quality our staff have is passion. Our coaches love to paddle just as much as you do. On their day off you'll find every one of them out on the water doing what they love most - paddling. We firmly believe that their unique blend of experience and enthusiasm makes us the number one choice for skills development.

So whether you'd like to improve your white water, freestyle, sea paddling, canoeing, or even your roll, make sure you benefit from our experience.

For a brochure call 01690 720214 or e-mail brochure @pyb.co.uk

PLAS Y BRENIN

Canolfan Fynydd Genedlaethol · The National Mountain Centre

Capel Curig Conwy LL24 OET Tel: 01690 720214 Fax: 01690 720394 www.pyb.co.uk Email: info@pyb.co.uk

Kayak Rolling / Pesda Press

SWIMMING POOL GAMES

Probably the ideal time and place to introduce paddling is on a sheltered small lake on a warm summer s day, however the vagaries of the weather rarely afford us this luxury. One way of overcoming this is to use a swimming pool - it s often a great place in which to be introduced to kayaking and canoeing - as it's warm, clean, a controlled environment, and available all year round.

Whilst the games outlined in this section are ideal for the swimming pool, that doesn t mean that with the right preparation they cannot be played on a summer s day on sheltered water. Conversely it s true that the swimming pool is an ideal warm environment for lots of tippy, wet games which you might not enjoy or even try on a cold day. Also, the confined playing area of a pool helps to keep a game together - in the game 'Hacky thump', for example, the fun would be lost if all the participants could spread out as far as they wished; the controlled playing field offers the maximum chance of being caught.

One of the great things about a swimming pool is that it is a warm and friendly place so ideal to take away the fears of the first capsize. With modern boats that have large cockpits (or sit on tops) a formal capsize drill is often unnecessary - a good clear brief and some dry land based games may be all that s needed. The luxury of a warm, indoor pool and a few water confidence games will allow you introduce capsize as a fun possibility - NOT a cold wet inevitability!

Modern plastic kayaks, canoes and sit on tops can all be safely used in swimming pools with minimum risk of damage (see the BCU leaflet that is available). There are however some special considerations:

Do please respect the pool with the equipment you are using.

- **Wash your boats** and other equipment before you bringing them into the pool. (Check this out with the pool management)

- Take care when carrying or emptying boats not to damage tiles, etc. (very rare in our experience) and don t flood the attendant's office!

- Ask before you hang up ropes , or bring in other equipment.

- Think carefully about the **use of paddles.** If the game requires paddles then it also probably needs helmets and buoyancy aids.

- A basic safety rule is that if people are moving around with paddles then there should be **no swimming** or wading in the water.

- If you have to share the pool with other users then take special care - the pool will need to roped off to prevent other users entering the paddling area. Also avoid playing boisterous games which involve paddling fast or which run a risk of one of your boats going out of your zone and hitting a swimmer.

- Pool time is normally expensive, so plan ahead as to how you can maximise the experience. A good format is to have **two people to each boat.** This is good for the learning experience, speeds up the logistics, and many of our pool games are based on this.

Kayah Rolling / Pesda Press

SWIMMING POOL GAMES

WATER CONFIDENCE

Game	Boat	Skill Development.	Level	Strokes	Good?
30. Ship wreck	CKS	Water confidence, balance, spatial awareness, twisting, stretching, timing, agility, co-ordination and cooperation.	1	N/A	▯▯▯
31. Pick up	CKS	As above.	1	N/A	▯▯▯
32. Porpoising	CKS	As above + orientation.	1	N/A	▯▯▯
33. Kayak wrestling	CKS	As above	1	N/A	▯▯▯
34. Crocodile wrestling	CKS	As above	1	N/A	▯▯▯
35. Roly-Poly	CKS	As above.	1	N/A	▯▯▯
36. Getting in	CKS	As above	1	N/A	▯▯▯
37. Getting out	CKS	As above	1	N/A	▯▯
38. Introduction to capsize	CKS	As above	1	Capsize Drill	▯▯
39. All capsize	CKS	As above	1	Capsize Drill Swim	▯▯
40. Empty out	CKS	As above	1	Lifting technique	▯

OTHER POOL GAMES

Game	Boat	Skill Development.	Level	Strokes	Good?
45. Hacky thump	CKS	Balance, active posture, control, rotation.	1	N/A	▯▯▯
46. Bingo	CKS	Control, balance, co-ordination, turning, vision, pacing.	1-2	Various	▯▯
47. Paddle racing	--	Power transition, push/pulling, co-ordination	1	N/A	▯▯
48. Aqua-kayaking	CKS	Water confidence, spatial awareness.	1	N/A	▯▯
49. Cowboys and Indians	K	Balance, control, reaction, dynamic posture, bracing.	1-4	N/A	▯▯▯
50. Dolphins	K	Balance, control, reaction, dynamic posture, bracing.	1-4	N/A	▯▯▯
51. Duck races	CKS	Control, balance, turning, balance, speed.	1-3	Various	▯▯
52. Prui	KS	Control, feeling, balance, turning, reaction.	1-3	Various	▯▯▯

ROLLING GAMES

Game	Boat	Skill Development.	Level	Strokes	Good?
55. Rolling tag	K	Co-ordination, flexibility, control, balance, orientation and rotation.	3-5	Rolls	▯▯
56. Swim and roll up game	K	As above.	3-5	Rolls	▯▯
57. Rolling Relay	K	As above.	3-5	Rolls	▯▯
58. Kayak swap	K	As above.	3-5	Rolls	▯▯

DRY = Dry Land Game

DAMP = Afloat but should stay dry

WET = Some chance of splashing and accidental capsize

SWIM = High probability of a swim or similar

Water confidence is so important, and a real key to learning to paddle, an ability to swim is NOT. Here s a few games to help develop water confidence.

CKS

BALLS, ETC

30 Ship wreck — Level 1

Here is a good game to start with. Prior to the session float the boats in the pool, one boat for every 2-3 people then also throw in some buoyancy aids, a few footballs, tennis balls and swimming. Have your group get into the pool, each small group has to collect all the flotsam around them and put it in their boats. They all have to keep hold of their group s boat. The groups can swim or wade. *Loel Collins*

CKS

LOTS OF BALLS

31 Pick up — Level 1

You need a large bag of plastic balls, 100 s of red, blue, green and yellow. With the boats in the pool the groups split into teams and have to collect the balls and put them into their boats, different colour boats for different colour balls or a certain number of balls, or one of each colour. At the end of the game I tend to leave the balls in the pool and then play clear up game at the end of the session. *Loel Collins*

CKS

32 Porpoising — Level 1

Get some of the group to hold the boats still and then have the rest of the group dive under the first, climb over the second, under the next etc, it s good fun and reminds us that getting our head wet is no big deal!

Loel Collins

33 Kayak wrestling
Level 1   CKS

Split your group into pairs. Stand in the shallow end on different sides of a boat and facing each. The idea is to wrestle the kayak towards you. Reach across the boat to the opposite edge and wrestle it over, whilst the other person does the same, best of three counts as the winner.

Loel Collins

34 Crocodile wrestling
Level 1   CKS

I learnt this off crocodile Dundee when he was working as a nature walk instructor at Plas y Brenin! With the boat, climb onto the back deck and get the boat in a big hug. Now you have to spin the boat round and round until the croc/boat or you have won.

Loel Collins

Kayak Rolling / Pesda Press

35 Roly Poly
Level 1   CKS

Named after Polly who let us try this on her and now we use it all the time for water confidence orientation and generally fun. Pair up, one person standing, the other tucked into a ball and floating just in front of their partner. The partner has to spin and tumble the float ball round and round, once the floater has had enough they simply stretch out and the tumbling will stop. This is always good for laugh and a great one for water confidence!

Loel Collins

CKS

 CKS

 CKS

Capsize Drill

36 Getting in
Level 1

Have everyone in the pool and then try getting your group to climb into the boats, from the stern, over the side or any way they want. This always ends in a capsize and lots of splashing and falling around. Let each person choose how how they want to sit in the boat, legs, in, out, knees up, knees down.
Loel Collins

37 Getting out
Level 1

Then, after all that effort, try getting out without capsizing the boats or going to the side.
Loel Collins

38 Introduction to capsizing
Level 1

If people are happy to, It is often better to cover a capsize as and when the opportunity arises. However, if you prefer, here is a progression of simple games to ease the nerves and introduce the idea of capsizing as being safe and fun. These are best done with either a coach or a partner standing by the boat.

1. Have each person sit on the boat with their legs outside the cockpit and then try to tip the boat over - they will invariably fall off the kayak.
2. Then try the same and capsize with feet in the cockpit but knees up. It will usually be the same result.
3. Then, after a demo from you, capsize with knees in the cockpit, but sitting in an un-braced position.
4. Then capsize from a sitting braced position after a demo from you.
5. Then show the group the swimmer to boat rescue and have them try it on the boats without spay decks. The boats will sink

Kayak Rolling / Pesda Press

so you will also need to cover emptying boats if you haven t done so already.

6. Then with partners and after a demo from you, capsize with loose fitting decks but only just on at the front.

7. Then paired up and after a demo from you, with loose fitting/nylon decks. Before giving this a go try getting them to release the deck a couple of time, hand on head, eyes shut, left handed, right handed, holding your breath, before you actually have them go over. *Loel Collins*

39 All capsize   Level 1   CKS

Capsize Drill

Once the group has mastered capsizing both with and without a spray deck. get them to capsize individually and then all together. You will need some people on the side as look-outs. *Loel Collins*

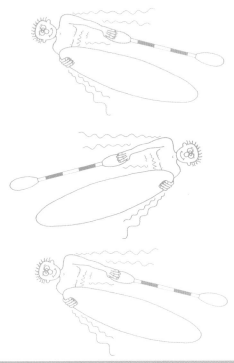

40 Empty out   Level 1   CKS

Lifting technique

It is important to do a clear demonstration of how to empty a boat. Boats fill with water and can be very heavy. Ideally all the boats should have airbags fitted and inflated. Have your group work together in pairs to empty boats and brief them about the correct technique for lifting the boats so as not to damage their backs.

Loel Collins

PIPE LAGGING

45 Hacky thump
Level 1

This is for people with more muscle than brains, like myself, and what little brain they have will be knocked out as well! Players in boats spread out over a given area. Hands are used to move around. The special piece of equipment required for this game is an old bit of foam pipe-lagging. Each player has one piece which is 1-2 feet long. The aim is simple: to hit whoever you can on the helmet. My Auntie Floss thinks that this is a horrid nasty game!

BALLS & DUCKS

46 Bingo
Level 1-2

This works well in a pool or in a confined area. Have a number of table tennis balls, or corks, or plastic ducks and number them and set them afloat. Call out a number the group paddles around and the first to find the number is the winner of that round, the one with the most numbers at the end of the session is the overall winner.

47 Paddle racing
Level 1

For a change, this game requires only a paddle. The basic idea is for everyone to stand up at the shallow end of the pool holding the paddle in the normal way. On the word 'Go!' they have to paddle forwards all the way to the other end of the pool. The first to arrive is the winner.

You can use the following variations:
1. Take both feet off the ground then paddle to the end.
2. Go across the width of the pool.
3. Float on your back with your feet in front and the paddle lying across your stomach. Paddle towards your feet.
4. Draw-stroke up the pool with the paddle in front of your body.

CKS

48 Aqua-kayaking
Level 1

As an instructor I tell children off for doing this, as it is hard to tell if they are just playing in an upside-down boat or if they might be in trouble. However, since kids love to play it, I do it in a controlled situation. Players work in partners and have one kayak between the two. They turn the kayak upside-down and then, one at a time, put their head inside the cockpit and sing a song. This game must be carefully supervised.

TEAM GAMES for the pool

Polo - See Polo and Ball Games, Chapter 3.

Kayak Polo is one of the most popular swimming pool games and is played all over the world. Before you play it, consider the size of your pool, control and safety issues. For most smaller pools, it is better not to use paddles - use hands only and have some people ready on the pool side ready to jump in and do a swimmer to kayak rescue in the event of a capsize.

Blindfold polo

A great game for the swimming pool - see number 73 in the next chapter.

49 Cowboys and Indians   Level 1   K

Split the group into two teams of equal number. Decide on a given area to play within. One team is called the Indians and the other the Cowboys (and Cowgirls!). The idea is for one team to capsize the other. Send each team to opposite ends and get them to face one another for the ensuing battle. To make it a little bit more interesting both sides have to sit on the backs of the decks with their feet on the seats. This will make it very tippy and more fun. Floats or hands should be used instead of paddles.

K

50 Dolphins
Level 1

This is a fun game and it is not as rough as it sounds. Get as many people as possible to play. Everybody spreads out over the pool. For safety reasons no paddles are allowed. On the word 'Go!' everybody has to turn as many other players over as they can. If a player is turned over and there are two or more players still upright then they are allowed to empty out and rejoin the game. The winner is the last one left upright. It is important that this game is carefully supervised.

 CKS

DUCKS

51 Duck races
Level 1

If you think about it, a swimming pool is just like an extra large bath. If you happen to come across ten yellow plastic ducks in this bath, you could fill the whole session with duck games. Here are some ideas.
- Balance the duck on the front of the boat and do a length.
- Balance the duck on your head.
- Dribble the duck.
- Collect the ducks.

I was once offered 2000 small plastic yellow duck left over from a charity duck race, we filled the pool with them and had a great time; hunting them out, playing hide and seek, and herding them like duck dogs.

 KS

BLIND FOLDS

52 Prui
Level 1

Each player is blindfolded. No paddles are to be used. The idea is for all the players to move around the water trying to find the 'Prui', a person secretly chosen by the leader. The Prui has no blindfold. Every time a player bumps into another player they have to shake hands and say 'Prui'. If the other person is not the Prui they also say 'Prui', then both move on. When a player bumps into the real Prui the Prui stays quiet and the two join hands. The next person to bump into the Prui raft joins it. until one big raft is created. Players forming part of the Prui raft can take off the blindfold and watch the others shaking hands and saying 'Prui'. Players can also vary the way they say 'Prui' - they may whisper or shout, for example.

There are many different kinds of rolling games, some for individuals, some for teams. They are all useful for practising and developing good technique.

- **You can invent** many different types of game incorporating rolling. Here are a few ideas.
- How many rolls can the players do non-stop?
- How many rolls can they do in a minute or other given time?
- How many different rolls can they do without repeating the same one?
- You can have variations on a roll, for example right, left, back or front.
- How good is the group at synchronised rolling?
- How long does it take to do a hundred rolls?

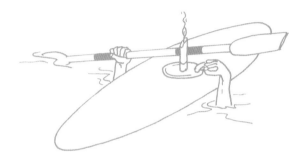

55 Rolling tag   Level 3-5   K

Rolls

In this game you need a minimum of two players, but about six would be best. Make sure everyone has enough space to roll in, then give each player a number. No. I starts by doing one roll. No. 2 then has to do the same roll and add one more. The game continues in this manner until a paddler fails to do the roll properly or cannot think of a different roll to do. The rolls have to be done in the same order each time. The winner is the one left.

56 Swim and roll up game   Level 3-5   K

Rolls

The idea of this game is to swim to an upside-down kayak, get in it and then roll up. Have all the kayaks turned over with the paddles in the cockpits. Make sure there is not too much water in them. Push the kayaks out. On the word 'Go!' all the paddlers jump into the pool and swim underwater until they get to a kayak. Then they pull the paddle out, take a breath of air from the cockpit, get into the kayak and roll up. There is no need to put a spraydeck on. Paddles or hands can be used to roll up. The first one up wins.

Rolls

57 Rolling Relay — Level 1

This can be a team race or just one exercise. Place boats in a line side by side, quite close to each other, with just one paddle per team. The first (who has the paddle) and second boats capsize, first rolls up and passes paddle across to two (who is still capsized), when first rolls up third capsizes, second rolls up (four capsizes) and passes paddle to third, and so on to the end of the line. If this is a race then the winners are the first team to have everybody rolled up.

Bob Walker

Kayak Rolling / Pesda Press

Rolls

58 Underwater kayak swap — Level 1

This game is best done initially with two people, introducing more players when the skills are mastered. The idea is to turn over and swap kayaks without breaking the surface for air.

SWIMMING POOL

Kayak Rolling

- the Black Art Demystified

a great book on rolling

Bang up to date

ISBN 0-95311956-8-6

www.pesdapress.com

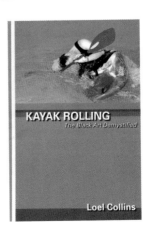

To make paddling courses easier, we've introduced multiple choice.

This year we're running more courses, on more dates, than ever before. Making it simpler for you to choose a date that fits in with your schedule. And because we're busier than we've ever been, when you get here you'll find the atmosphere's great too.

What's more, our unique position makes it easier to choose the right spot every time. Nestled deep in the mountains of Snowdonia, we have the perfect location with a huge choice of venues all around us. There are countless classic runs on the Dee, Llugwy, Conwy, Glaslyn, Ogwen and Lledr along with plenty of hidden gems, many of which our staff can claim as first descents.

For the sea paddlers countless classic sea trips are within easy reach too including The Skerries, South Stacks and Bardsey island. This variety allows us to tailor each course to suit your ability, taking into account the weather conditions and water levels. Which means you're guaranteed the best possible learning experience.

So when it comes to deciding where to go on a paddling course, you'll find there is no decision to be made.

Plas y Brenin is the right choice every single time.

For a free 56-page colour brochure telephone 01690 720214 or e-mail brochure@pyb.co.uk

PLAS Y BRENIN

Canolfan Fynydd Genedlaethol · The National Mountain Centre

Capel Curig Conwy LL24 OET Tel: 01690 720214 Fax: 01690 720394 www.pyb.co.uk Email: info@pyb.co.uk

Lou Manouch

POLO & BALL GAMES

Game	Boat	Skill Development.	Level	Stroke	Good?
60. Catch	CKS	Active posture, dynamic balance, reaction, bracing, rotation, turning, bending, power transfer, start and stop, spatial awareness, communication and vison.	1-3	N/A	‖
61. Keep that ball up	CKS	As above	1-3	N/A	‖
62. Moose Ball	CKS	As above	1-3	Various	‖
63. Basic Polo	CKS	As above	2-4	Various	‖‖
64. Hands only	CKS	As above	2-4	Various	‖
65. Central goal	CKS	As above	2-4	Various	‖‖
66. Inner tube as goal	CKS	As above	2-4	Various	‖
67. Bucket as a goal	CKS	As above	2-4	Various	‖‖
68. No goals	CKS	As above	2-4	Various	‖
69. Balloon	CKS	As above	2-4	Various	‖
70. Beach ball	CKS	As above	2-4	Various	‖
71. Fitness ball	CKS	As above	2-4	Various	‖‖
72. Pass the ball	CKS	As above	2-4	Various	‖
73. Blindfold Polo	CKS	As above	2-4	Various	‖‖
74. Water netball	CKS	As above	2-4	Various	‖‖
75. Soft ball	CKS	As above	2-4	Various	‖

DRY = Dry Land Game

DAMP = Afloat but should stay dry

WET = Some chance of splashing and accidental capsize

SWIM = High probability of a swim or similar

60 Catch

Level 1-3   CKS

BALLS

Play a simple game of catch with the boats spaced out in a rough circle, with either 1, 2 or even three balls. The thrower must call out the name of the person they are throwing to.

Plas y Brenin - www.pyb.co.uk

61 Keep that ball up

Level 1-3   CKS

BALL

This came from an unsuccessful attempt at playing volleyball from canoes. In this game players have a ball or balloon. They get as close as possible without forming a raft and, using hands only, try to keep the ball in the air. You could count how many times the ball has been hit up and then try to beat the club record.   *Dave Rossetter*

62 Moose Ball

Level 1-3   CKS

BALL

This game needs two teams and one soft ball. You score if you can pass to a member of your team over the top of someone on the opposite team. (so your team mates have to keep moving to put the opposition in the way). Two points are scored if two people are in between, etc. This seems to be one of those games that everyone just wants to keep playing for ages.   *Kath Wright*

Kayak polo is a game that is unique, exciting and fun. Almost everyone who learns to paddle will play one of its versions at some time in their formative years and at more serious levels it is played by thousands of people around the world, in local, national and international competitions. Many versions of Polo can be played in both canoes and kayaks.

Kayak Polo games can get pretty physical. This raises several **safety** issues for the coach, some can be dealt with in the game briefing and some will require careful monitoring while the game in progress.

1. Because of the danger of collisions, Polo games are not normally suitable for beginners.
2. Warn of the danger of collisions, & brief paddlers how to avoid them.
3. Use only boats with broad rounded ends.
4. Ensure paddles have no sharp edges.
5. Ensure Buoyancy aids are pulled down and fit snugly.
6. Wear Helmets.
7. Define the playing area and goals.
8. Balls not to be carried in the cockpit of kayaks (entrapment danger).
9. Ensure your have a way of stopping the game (a **whistle** works well).

Sometimes it s tempting for the coach to get involved with the game and with care you could perhaps enter the game to spur things along, however great care should be taken not to compromise safety and control.

BALL CKS

63 Basic polo

Level 2-4

At a recreational level we suggest these rules -

1. Two teams.
2. Two goals.
3. Switch ends at half time.
4. No holding the ball.
5. No carrying the ball.
6. No capsizing opponents.
7. No pushing or pulling opponents.

Plas y Brenin - www.pyb.co.uk

8. No ramming or collisions.
9. No hitting the ball with the paddle.
10. Penalty shots and red cards for foul play.

64 Hands only
Level 2-4

CKS
BALL

Play polo as above, but without paddles - this is a great idea for a swimming pool or a smaller playing area on a warm day. This makes the game safer with less risk of injury and perhaps you don't need to wear helmets? Brief the players what to do in the event that someone capsizes. Perhaps you need rescuers on the bank, ready to jump in and do a swimmer to boat rescue?

Plas y Brenin - www.pyb.co.uk

65 Central goal
Level 2-4

CKS
BALL

This variant focuses the game to a central point and makes the boundaries less important. If the coach's boat is the goal, then it's easy to keep the score! You can also make this into a journey game and slowly move the group say down the river.

66 Inner tube as a goal
Level 1-3

CKS
BALL & INNER TUBE

Use a large inner tube (a tractor one is great) - either floating around so the ball has to lobbed into it, or tethered on it's side so the ball has to be thrown through the hole.

67 Bucket as a goal
Level 2-4

CKS
BALL, BUCKETS & INNERTUBES

Use a bucket suspended in a small inner tube and the game becomes basket ball! Use different coloured buckets and cut holes in the bottom of them so they don't float.

II CKS
BALL

68 No Goals
Level 2-4

The group is split into equal teams. Team members have to pass a ball between one another without dropping it, the opposition try to win possession by intercepting. The ball can only be retained for 3 seconds before making a pass. A number of clean successive passes should be set as a target to either score a point or win the game.

Dave Williams

Plas y Brenin - www.pyb.co.uk

II CKS
BALLOONS

69 Balloon polo
Level 2-4

This is played as basic polo, but play using a balloon. It is best played on calm days with a smaller playing area. The game becomes slow and graceful. Tip try putting a little water in the balloon and note the difference in play.

II CKS
BEACH BALLS

70 Beach ball polo
Level 2-4

Use a large beach ball this is an ideal game for canoes. When played with kayaks, a plus point is that if it the ball is big enough, then it can t get into the cockpits to trap people. It s a happy mid-ground between using a balloon and using a basket ball.

III K
FITNES BALL

71 Fitness ball
Level 2-4

Try and borrow one of those big fitness balls (around 60cm diameter) and play polo with this. Brief players that the ball cannot be lifted or thrown - it has to be pushed around with either the boats or hands. Best played without paddles, a larger playing area is often better on calm warm days.

Lou Manouch

72 Pass the ball
Level 2-4

CKS
BALL

The ball has to be passed to **every paddler** in the team before a goal can be scored. This is a very useful variant if you have teams with widely differing skill levels and encourages complete group participation.
Caroline Gerritsen

73 Blindfold Polo
Level 2-4

CKS
BALL & BLINDFOLDS

Blindfold the group and split it into two teams, one at each end of the pool. Use hands only in case someone gets hit in the face by a paddle Otherwise the rules can be much the same as for normal polo, but accidental bumping into one another is allowed. Each team has an external player who is on the bank or poolside and does not wear a blindfold - their job is to call out instructions to their team, telling them where the ball is and in what direction to throw it. The external player is not allowed to touch the ball. Another alternative is to use a ball with bells in it so players can hear where the ball is. The goals can be any of the ideas above.

74 Water netball
Level 2-4

CKS
BALL & HOOP OR NET

This is similar to land netball but played on the water. Have a set playing area with a net at both ends. Moving with the ball is not allowed. The game can be played with paddles or just hands. Pick teams of fairly equal ability, as too many good players on one side will destroy the fun. The game can be played with no physical contact for beginners or perhaps anything goes in the case of more competent paddlers! If there are no fixed nets you could use a boat at each end, with the cockpit as the goal.

Alternatively, you could use a hoop or the net that the pool attendant uses to pick the rubbish out of the pool as a hand-held net. The referee has to catch the ball for both teams, changing ends each time a goal has been scored. If you are on a lake and only have the use of one bank, the referee can throw the ball as far as possible; each team then races out to bring it back and try for the net.   Other variations are:

1. Two teams play against each other
   with one or two nets.
2. Three teams or more play.
3. Play as one group by passing and shooting.
4. Use two or more balls and perhaps
   a Frisbee as well. *Plas y Brenin - www.pyb.co.uk*

POLO & BALL GAMES

The instructor divides the group into two, one team batting and the other fielding. The instructor is normally the bowler for both sides. The bowler is about 2 metres away from the batter, who, if possible, is in front of a wall or bank of some sort. The game is played like a normal game of soft ball or rounders, but boats simply paddle around the bowler to score. If a player misses the ball three times they are out. Use a soft ball for this game; the paddle is the bat.

TAG GAMES

Many versions of tag games can be played in both canoes and kayaks, however, games of this nature can get pretty physical. This raises several safety issues for the coach - some can be dealt with by a clear game briefing and some will require careful monitoring whilst the game is in progress.

1. Because of the danger of collisions, Tag games are not normally suitable for beginners.

2. Warn of the danger of collisions, and brief paddlers how to avoid them.

3. Use only boats with broad rounded ends.

4. Ensure paddles have no sharp edges.

5. Ensure buoyancy aids are pulled down and fit snugly.

6. Wear Helmets.

7. Clearly define the playing area.

8. Ensure you have a way of stopping the game (a whistle works well).

9. Dont use paddles to tag people or boats - There is a danger of a paddle in someones face. It is safer if the person on or It has to physically touch the boat or person.

10. It is usually best to select a strong paddler to be it at the start of the game.

Sometimes its tempting for the coach to get involved with the game and with care you could perhaps enter the game to spur things along, however great care should be taken not to compromise safety and control.

TAG GAMES

Game	Boat	Skill Development.	Level	Stroke	Good?
80. Basic tag	CKS	Speed, pace control, acceleration, balance, control, power transfer, reaction, vision, spatial awareness.	2-4	Various	❚❚❚
81. Hands Only tag	CKS	As above + co-ordination.	2-4	Hand paddling	❚❚
82. Team tag	CKS	As above, tactics and teamwork.	2-4	Various	❚❚❚
83. Simpsons tag	CKS	As above, tactics and teamwork.	2-4	Various	❚❚❚
84. Ball tag	CKS	As above + co-ordination.	2-4	Various	❚❚❚
85. Sponge tag	CKS	As above + co-ordination.	2-4	Various	❚❚❚
86. Plunger tag	CKS	As above + deceleration.	2-4	Various	❚❚❚
87. Nukeomb ball	CKS	As above.	2-4	Various	❚❚
88. Sharks & Dolphins	CKS	As above.	2-4	Various	❚❚
89. Titanic tag	CKS	As above.	2-4	Various	❚❚
90. Kiss Me tag	CKS	As above.	2-4	Various	❚❚
91. Pin the Tail on the donkey	CKS	As above.	2-4	Various	❚❚
92. Pick Pocket	CKS	As above.	2-4	Various	❚❚
93. Buccaneer tag	CKS	As above.	2-4	Various	❚❚
94. Freeze tag	CKS	As above.	2-4	Various	❚❚
95. Balloon tag	CKS	As above + boat agility.	2-4	Various	❚❚❚
96. Blindfold Rattler	CKS	As above.	2-4	Hand paddling	❚❚
97. Hare and hounds	CKS	As above.	2-4	Various	❚❚
98. Dragon s Den	CKS	Control, posture, balance, vision, reaction, planning.	1-2	Various	❚❚❚
99. Escort	K	Active posture, turning, reaction,	1-2	Hand paddling	❚❚

DRY = Dry Land Game

DAMP = Afloat but should stay dry

WET = Some chance of splashing and accidental capsize

SWIM = High probability of a swim or similar

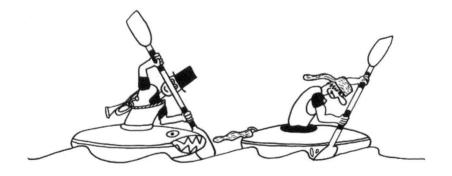

80 Basic Tag

Level 2-4   CKS

One person is on - called It and has to chase the other members of the group and tag them by tapping the back of their boats with their hand 3 times. That person then becomes it and the game continues.

81 Hands Only Tag

Level 2-4   CKS

As above but without paddles, and a great idea for a swimming pool or a smaller playing area on a warm day. This probably makes the game safer with less risk of injury and perhaps you don t need to wear helmets?

Plas y Brenin - www.pyb.co.uk

82 Team Tag

Level 2-4   CKS

This is the same as basic tag, above, but when a person is tagged they join It as part of the tagged team and they then play as a team gradually tagging more people to form a larger and larger team.

83 Simpsons Tag

Level 2-4   CKS

As Team Tag but the chaser (It) has to shout Doe just like Homer and until they are caught all paddlers shout Eat my shorts just like Bart. If your group are not into the Simpsons then change the characters -perhaps animals and noises? This adds quite a bit of fun to the basic game.

Geoff Barrett

III CKS

BALL

84 Ball Tag   Level 2-4

A variation is to hit the boat with a soft ball. Decide if the paddlers are able to deflect the ball from hitting their boat with hands or paddle and whether those who are on can or cannot paddle with the ball.

Dave Williams

Lou Manouch

III CKS

SPONGE

85 Sponge Tag   Level 2-4

This is the same as the previous game but using a nice wet sponge!.

III CKS

SINK PLUNGER

86 Plunger Tag   Level 2-4

Use a small sink plunger to play tag, you need to check that the craft have enough flat areas for the plungers to stick. A variation is for each craft to have a plunger and everyone has to try to collect as many plungers as they can. The winner has the most plungers.   *Loel Collins*

II CKS

BALLS

87 Nukeomb Ball   Level 2-4

This game needs several small footballs, sponges, or something similar. The coach throws the toys out for all to chase. Once you have one you must not paddle with it but throw it at an opponent. You get two points for the body and one point for the boat (or whatever scoring you want to adopt)

Dave Rosseter

Lou Manouch

You need a well defined playing area such as a wide stretch of river (at least 25m or more) and two ends, banks, or similar home areas where the players are safe from being tagged—normally they cannot be caught if they are close to, or touching the bank or ends.

To start with, one player is on (called sharky) who sits in the middle of the playing area waiting. Everyone else spreads out along the bank ready to try & paddle across. Sharky shouts GO & then they have to make it to the opposite "home" without being tagged. You get tagged if sharky touches the back of your boat (from cockpit to the stern). If you are tagged then you are eaten & you become a shark too. So the numbers of sharks steadily grows until only one dolphin is left who then becomes the winner and the next shark.

Safety Briefing

Before playing this game we always brief groups on how to avoid an incoming kayak bow going straight for your ribs/kidneys.

Paddling backwards or forwards to avoid is popular! As a last resort we demonstrate how easy it is to push the incoming nose of kayak away with ones hand. It requires no physical strength and can even be done with one mighty "finger of power" (instructor demonstrates but emphasises that using a whole hand is better!). We stress not trying to stop the kayaks momentum which leads to crushed fingers! Ouch! Kayaks riding over the cockpit is not a major problem (see demonstration) so no need to panic!

Mathew Bishop   Lou Manouch

CKS

89 Titanic Tag
Level 2-4

A rectangular area is defined as Bow, Stern, Port (left), Starboard (right), one of these is called out by whoever is running the game and the paddlers have to make it to the boundary without being intercepted and tagged by the person/s who is "it". Anyone tagged also becomes it until only one person remains.

Dave Williams

CKS

90 Kiss Me Tag
Level 2-4

This game is widely played in the school playgrounds and on the street but I am not sure if it has been adapted for paddling. Why not—with the right group this could be just the added spice you need? No special equipment is needed but I do recommend that both sexes are involved, unless you have very modern ideas. One person is 'on' and they have to try and kiss another, who is then 'on'. The others shout Kiss me and are supposed to try and not to get caught.

CKS

PEGS

91 Pin The Tail On The Donkey
Level 2-4

The person who is It has a handful of large pegs (or bits of pipe lagging) and each peg has a bit of bright tape tied to it. The person who is on It has to catch the rest by pinning the clothes peg to the stern handle of the others boats — pinning the tail onto the donkeys. The game is complete when all the donkeys have tails.

Once the game is complete the next game is for the players it to collect all the tails back again without losing their own.

Loel Collins

92 Pick Pocket

Level 2-4   CKS

Background note: my country town of Hexham, on the banks of the Tyne, has a market dating back to the 13th Century and once had a bad reputation for pickpockets.

All paddlers assemble in the centre of the river and discuss the price of geese, cabbages etc as if they were in the market in the Middle Ages. They also solemnly warn each other of the possible presence of pickpockets. One paddler, previously selected to be the pickpocket, circles the group slowly one or twice. Without warning he taps someone's boat and makes off as fast as possible in any direction. The person, whose boat has been tapped shouts, "Stop thief !" and all paddlers in the group chase the 'thief wherever he goes until one taps the thief s canoe. That person then becomes the next pickpocket and the game starts again.

Paul Burgess, Hexham Canoe Club

Plas y Brenin - www.pyb.co.uk

93 Buccaneer Tag

Level 2-4   CKS

This game takes place in the open where there are lots of small islands or rocks. Mark out a starting and a finishing line behind which players are safe. Players have to get from the start to the finish, racing round the islands, without being caught and tagged by the buccaneers. At least two buccaneers are 'on', while the rest of the group play the part of decent respectable people sailing across the sea. Once a player is 'had' they become a buccaneer.

Once players get across the finishing line they and the other survivors line up and get ready to go again. For safety reasons the islands must be small so that the players are not out of sight. Another idea would be that every player has to carry a leaf (instead of jewels) and. to be 'had', have the leaf taken from them.

94 Freeze Tag

Level 2-4

Select 2-3 persons to be it simultaneously, depending on the size of the group. When a victim is tagged they become "frozen" and sit with their paddle on their head. They remain motionless unless someone who has not been tagged un-freezes them by touching their boat, they can then resume paddling. The game continues until all victims are "frozen". It restarts with the last three to be caught being 'it' for the second game.

Dave Williams

Plas Y Brenin - www.pyb.co.uk

 CKS

BALLOONS

95 Balloon Tag

Level 2-4

This is a good game for young beginners, and is particularly useful after a lesson in which you have been teaching turns and emergency stops. Each boat has a balloon tied to the back loop. Mark out a given area to play in. The idea is for players to chase all the others and burst their balloons without getting their own burst first. Watch out for ramming. This can be played by individuals or as follows:

1. by two teams
2. by several teams, each with a different-coloured balloon
3. by some players who have balloons and some who have sticks sharpened at one end. (The balloons are whales and the others are the whalers.)

II CKS

SOUND DEVICE
& BLINDFOLDS

96 Blindfold Rattler Tag

Level 2-4

The whole group is blindfolded except for the 'rattler', who must be caught. The rattler has an old tin with a few stones in it which must be rattled every 30 seconds so the others can hear it. When the rattler is caught the 'catcher' takes over. It is safer not to use paddles.

97 Hare & Hounds

Level 2-4   CKS

SPONGE OR
PIPE LAGGING

Delineate a set area in which to play. Stick a piece of pipe lagging or an a sponge on the back of a canoe. This is the hare. The idea is for the tagged hare to race off, chased by the dreaded hounds, till one of the hounds touches the back of the tagged canoe. The person who succeeds then has to be the hare. This is not a blood sport!

98 Dragon s Den

Level 1-2   CKS

A projecting part of the river bank is selected as the Dragon's Den. One paddler, possibly the youngest, is chosen as the dragon's victim and he/she waits for rescue in the den. Another paddler is chosen as the dragon whose task it is to patrol about 10 yards outside his den and who can prevent rescuers from approaching and freeing the victim by touching their boats with his hand.

All other paddlers wait, scattered, some distance from the dragon and his den. At the start of the game the rescuers seek an opportunity to sneak past or behind the 'dragon ' without themselves having their boats tapped by him/her. Anyone tapped joins the victim(s) waiting to be 'eaten' at the dragon's next meal. It adds spice if the victims shout, "Help !" in a pitiful voice every now and then.

Paul Burgess

99 Escort

Level 2-4   CKS

This game is best played hand paddling to avoid accidents with paddles. Two teams line up on opposite sides of a rectangular playing area. One team have a member who has a balloon attached to their stern. Their objective is to escort the paddler from one side of the area to the other without the opposition bursting the balloon. They score a point for each successful crossing. Once the balloon has been burst the roles are reversed with the attackers becoming the balloon escorts.

Dave Williams

Plas y Brenin - www.pyb.co.uk

FLAT WATER GAMES

This section contains games that are suitable for larger areas of flat water, the games outlined in the Swimming Pool chapter could equally apply in this section providing the conditions are appropriate.

Flat water is where we all start, it s where we develop our foundation skills, so there is no need to turn your nose up at flat water, as there are more things to do and play in it than in any other type of water.

Nearly every area around the country has flat water close at hand. The only variations with flat water are that it can be warm, cold, clean, dirty or merely filthy. All types are usable, you just have to

pick a suitable game - tippy or not tippy. There is something for all: beginners can learn; experts can ease off and have fun by trying a silly game; competitors can use the flat to tidy up their stroke and for speed work-outs. Make the most of what you have on your doorstep - some people have no water at all.

Blindfolds can be used to add interest to many of these games, or simply used to give added awareness to a particular stroke or task. Use a 'sighted' person if necessary to call out directions to the teams or individuals. Most blindfold games are of course, much safer without paddles.

FLAT WATER GAMES

Game	Boat	Skill Development.	Level	Stroke	Good?
110. Disco Kings / Queens	CKS	Active posture, balance, rotation, lower body independence, co-ordination.	1-5	N/A	⫿⫿⫿
111. Midships	CKS	Co-ordination, timing, planning, speed, control, awareness.	2-3	Various.	⫿
112. Square Dance	KC	Balance, rotation, control, turning, reaction, power transfer.	1-3	Various	⫿
113. Listen to the Leader	CKS	Feeling, reaction, active posture, gliding, sliding, push/pull, turning, balance.	2-4	Various	⫿⫿
114. Low Brace Mexican Wave	CKS	Balance, dynamic posture, reaction, awareness.	2-4	Support strokes.	⫿
115. What's the time Mrs Wolf?	CKS	Balance, rotation, control, turning, reaction.	1-2	Sweep strokes	⫿
116. Salute the Admiral	CKS	Balance.	2-3	N/A	⫿
117. Digital numbers	CKS	Posture, rotation, control, turning, reaction.	1-2	Steering & draw strokes.	⫿
118. Syncronised paddling	CKS	Co-ordination, awareness, power transfer, control, reaction.	1-4	Various.	⫿⫿
119. Kayak Bridge	CKS	Control, speed, balance, push/pull, co-operation.	1-2	Stern rudder	⫿⫿⫿
120. Letter paddling	CKS	Balance, push/pull, control, power transfer.	1-2	Forward strokes	⫿
121. Evolution	CKS	Balance, rotation, control, turning, reaction, co-operation.	1-2	Various	⫿⫿
122. Animals & Film Stars	CKS	Imagination, posture, observation and acting skills.	1-2	Various	⫿⫿
123. Pararazzi	CKS	As above	1-2	Various	⫿⫿
124. Paddle Balancing	CKS	Balance, posture, rotation, edge, trim, stability, push/pull, power transfer.	1-3	N/A	⫿⫿
125. Snake Tails	CKS	Control, pace, awareness, reaction, timing.	1-3	Various	⫿⫿
126. Dragon Tails	CKS	Control, pace, awareness, reaction, timing.	1-3	Various	⫿⫿
127. Move to that spot	CKS	As above, pace control, acceleration and deceleration.	2-3	Various.	⫿
128. Lose that paddle	CKS	Balance, control, turning, awareness.	1-2	Hand paddling	⫿

PARTNER GAMES

Game	Boat	Skill Development.	Level	Stroke	Good?
140. Halt	CKS	Balance, rotation, control, turning, reaction, power transfer, glide.	2-3	Various	⫿⫿⫿
141. Greasy Pole	CKS	Balance, dynamic posture, reaction, awareness.	1-3	Various.	⫿⫿⫿
142. T Bone	KS	Active posture, balance, rotation, control, turning, reaction, power transfer.	1-2	Sweep strokes	⫿⫿
143. Head to Head	CKS	Pace control, reaction, push/pull, power transition, rotation.	2-3	Stern rudder	⫿⫿⫿
144. Guide Dogs	CKS	Feeling, reaction, active posture, gliding, sliding, push/pull, turning, balance, teamwork and communication.	2-4	Various	⫿⫿⫿

DRY = Dry Land Game

DAMP = Afloat but should stay dry

WET = Some chance of splashing and accidental capsize

SWIM = High probability of a swim or similar

Game	Boat	Skill Development.	Level	Stroke	Good?
TEAM GAMES					
150. Tug-of-war	CKS	Power transfer, push/pull, dynamic posture, reaction, awareness, use of core.	1-4	Forward paddling.	⫸⫸⫸
151. Sideways Tug of War	CKS	As above	2-4	Draw strokes	⫸⫸⫸
152. Backwards Tug of War	CKS	As above	1-4	Reverse paddling, emergency stopping.	⫸⫸⫸
153. Jousting	CKS	Balance, dynamic posture, reaction, awareness.	1-3	Various.	⫸⫸⫸
154. Sitting Ducks	CKS	Active posture, balance, power transfer, turning, reaction.	1-2	Various	⫸⫸
155. Throwline surf	CKS	Feel, speed, power transfer, control, balance, push/pull, reaction, co-operation.	1-3	Stern rudder, Support strokes.	⫸⫸⫸
156. Animal Farm	CKS	As above.	1-2	Various	⫸
157. Night Time Animals	CKS	As above.	1-2	Various	⫸⫸⫸
158. Switch	CKS	Co-ordination, awareness, power transfer, control, reaction.	1-4	Various.	⫸⫸
159. Darts	CKS	As above.	1-3	Stern rudder, Support strokes.	⫸⫸⫸

Plas Y Brenin - Disco Kings & Queens

CKS

110 Disco Kings & Queens
Level 1-5

At the start of a session get your group to use their hips etc. to rock the boat from side to side. This can then get be built up to include twisting with the upper body, leaning forward & back. Get groups in the mood by having music being played (you or the group singing can also work).

Dave Rosseter

CKS

111 Midships
Level 2-3

This game has many different names. Imagine that the area you have to play on is the deck of an old battleship. In our case it is water. One person is the caller who calls out things to do or places to go. The last paddler to do it is out. The last one left in the game is the caller in the next game. I have adapted the game to suit the water situation; you can add any of your own ideas. Here are some of mine.

1. The caller says port, starboard, bow or stern and every paddler has to rush in that direction.
2. Captains on deck . Everyone has to stand up in their boat. If players fall or are last they are out. They must salute when standing.
3. Freeze . Everyone stops dead still until the caller says 'Unfreeze!'. If the caller does not say 'Unfreeze!' but gives another command and the players move then they are out.
4. Row the boat . Everyone rafts up in pairs, then sits on the deck and starts to paddle around as in the game Chariots.
5. Island . Everyone makes one large raft; the last person is out.
6. Midships . Everyone paddles to the middle of the area. Last one to reach it is out.
7. Torpedoes . Spin the boat on the spot using forward and reverse sweeps.
8. Capsize boat . Everyone capsizes and re-enters solo.

Plas Y Brenin

112 Square Dance

Level 1-3   KC

Mark out a rectangle on the water with marker buoys or boats, say 20 metres apart. The group paddle around the rectangle, one by one, a reasonable distance apart. They paddle the first side of the square forward, the second left draw, third reverse and fourth right draw to complete the square. If there is enough room split into two groups and play as a team relay.   *Dave Williams*

113 Listen to the Leader

Level 2-4   CKS

BLINDFOLD

This is the same as 'Follow the leader' but. since the paddlers are blindfolded, they have to listen rather than look. The group all wear blindfolds except for the leader. The leader can lead from the boat or from the bank. There is no given area in this game; in fact. the further away players go the better. Everybody gets in their boat and awaits instructions. A good working number for the group would be from four to six. Have a rough idea as to where you are going but don't worry about improvising half-way through the game if you see something interesting. Here are some ideas you could use.

1. Paddle in a straight line.
2. Do 360¡ turns.
3. Get out of the boat alongside a high bank.
4. Carry your boat over a simple obstacle.
5. Re-enter your boat from a sloping bank.
6. Paddle backwards.
7. Use draw strokes, sweep strokes, etc.

Plas Y Brenin

114 Low Brace Mexican Wave

Level 2-4   CKS

Support strokes

The group either line up along side or sit in a circle and a Mexican wave effect (back and forth a couple of times) is performed using the desired stroke. It s great for practising the low brace, but can be used for other strokes and edging. The advantage of a game like this is no number or equipment restriction, no winners or losers and no problems if you re the strongest or weakest in the group.   *Nicky Marsh*

CKS

Sweep Strokes

115 What s the time Mrs Wolf? Level 1-2

The group moves out into a space large enough for each to perform a 360¡ turn. They call What s the time Mrs Wolf? to which the coach replies One o clock - and the group must perform one sweep stroke (probably a half turn), then 3 o clock , 6 o clock or whatever time the coach chooses until everyone is spinning on the spot like tops.

The game finishes when the coach suddenly calls out Dinner time! and the group must race home without being caught.   *Liz Beard*

CKS

116 Salute the Admiral Level 2-3

Here is one of those end-of-the-session games - that means time to get wet! It's a good game for a hot day after a successful lesson with new paddlers: you know they want a dip, so give it a go.

Get everybody to spread out so they are away from one another and the edge. Each paddler stands up in the boat and salutes - the aim is to get everybody standing up and saluting at the same time. To encourage them you could say that the world record is one fewer than the number in the group. You can be sure one person will fall in, and when that happens the others start to get legs like jelly. Before you know it they're all in. One point - keep your distance, as they will soon be swimming towards you to get revenge!

CKS

Various, steering and draw strokes

117 Digital numbers Level 1-2

Get the group to form numbers on the water. Using digital style numbers shout a number and get the group to form the shape (as if looking from above).

For example

One to Nine.

$$0\ 1\ 2\ 3\ 4$$
$$5\ 6\ 7\ 8\ 9$$

Andy Craven

118 Synchronised paddling

Level 1-4   CKS

This can be anything from making simple patterns, such as paddling behind each other keeping the line perfectly straight, or paddling a perfect circle with equally distanced boats to simple sequences such as a figure of eight (takes very careful distancing and timing at the cross point) or a synchronous hanging draw, to much more complicated things such as coordinated cartwheels.   *Caroline Gerritsen*

119 Kayak Bridge (Kayak Limbo and Daft Raft)   Level 1-3   CKS

Stern Rudder

Split the group into teams of 3 or more boats. Two kayaks sit parallel leaving a gap down the middle for another kayak to paddle through. A bridge is made from the paddles, by grasping them near the ends and holding them either in the air or across the cockpits. The paddler coming through the gap has either to glide under the bridge, doing a limbo, or has to stop, get out, climb over the bridge, and then get back in their boat and continue.   This is a great game for stern rudder practice.

Lou Manouch

120 Letter paddling

Level 1-2   CKS

Forward Strokes

Everybody lines up and a caller calls out one letter at a time. When a letter that is in a player's name is called they can take one paddle-stroke forwards. If the letter is in their name twice they take two paddle-strokes forwards. The person who gets to a pre-set line wins. If all the letters in their name have been called and the line has not yet been reached, they can start again from where they are. The winner becomes the caller.

FLAT WATER GAMES

121 Evolution
Level 1-2

This is a fun game with subtle learning and practice. Gather your group and explain that evolution is going from a lower life form to a higher one. Before starting decide on 4 or 5 life forms and associated noises, e.g:-

Snail   Slurp
Mouse   Squeek
Chicken   Cluck, Cluck
Dog   Woof, woof
Lion   Roar

The group all starts out as the lowest life form, e.g. a snail . The group paddle off and then each boat paddles around, making a slurping noise until they meet another snail.   When two identical life forms meet then they raft up and play Paper, scissors, rock—the winner evolves up one stage, the loser remains a humble snail.

On reaching the highest life form, the students have to either stand up or sit on the back deck, rear up like a lion and roar as loudly as possible. Adults will have a lot of fun deciding on more contentious life forms!

122 Animals and Film Stars

Get your group to imagine they are different animals and to imagine how that animal would paddle their boat! Let them have a go at paddling like a mouse, frog, giraffe, bumble bee, Gorilla etc Once they ve had a go. Get them to paddle past the group in the style of one of those animals, when the group recognised the animal they have to make the animals noise. Mouse eeK eeK , Giraffe, Gorilla, Frog, Bumble Bee, avoid donkey!! You can play the same game with famous film stars but the group then have to impersonate them, Marylyn Monroe happy birthday Mr President . Arnold Schwartaniger I ll be back .   *Loel Collins*

PGL Travel

123 Paparazzi

If you've played the film star version above, the next stage is to accept BLINDFOLDS
your Oscar, You have to walk down the red carpet with the photographers
and press shouting for the shot or interview. Split your group to form two
lines about 10-15m apart. The red carpet runs between the two columns,
each film star has to paddle down the red carpet. Decide in advance who
the lucky Paparazzi is, as the film star passes them they wave at the person
and they turn towards them and paddle over.

Of course, the bigger the film star the more practiced they are at ignoring
the unwanted intrusions of the press, so they wear dark classes (blind
fold). This time the paparazzi has to call at the film star to get them to turn
towards them.   *Loel Collins*

124 Paddling Balancing   Level 1-3   CKS

Suspend a paddle just above water level, from a tree or beam. Tie the rope   ROPE & SUPPORT
so the paddle is supported just at the ends of the loom, like a trapeze.
People can come up to the trapeze and try moving the boat forwards and
backwards, then side to side (with out putting the paddle in the water),
the trick is to imagine you are working in slow motion!. A really good test
is to try to get the boat balanced on its edge, left or right, but trying to
keep the ropes slack.   *Loel Collins*

Kayah Rolling / Pesda Press

ROPE

125 Snake tails

Attach a 10m length of floating line to the back of the snakes boat so that it trails behind them as they paddle. The rest of the group have to try and follow the tail. Make the snakes tails as long as you need or a short as you want!

Loel Collins

ROPE & RIBBONS

126 Dragon tails   Level 1

As above but tie a ribbon, sponge, etc. into the end of the tail so that it can be snatched out. The hobbits have to creep up onto the dragon and collect as many ribbons as possible. Of course dragons have to roar - but what noise do hobbits make?

Loel Collins

CKS

127 Move to that spot   Level 2-3

Define an area to play in. Tell all the players to spread out and find a spot at which to stop. Tell them to look for a new spot to move to when you say 'Go!'. When they have chosen one they must look at it non-stop. They should not look at other paddlers to see where they are looking, but move directly to their spot in a straight line. The aim is to get there without stopping or turning. They are allowed to alter speed. If they touch another boat, or have to stop, or turn, they are disqualified. You must decide whether or not players can use paddles.

CKS

Hand Paddling

128 Lose that paddle   Level 1-2

In this game everybody comes over to a spot on the bank where their paddles are taken away. The paddles are taken along the bank and all except one are thrown out to the deep waters. Players then have to get to a paddle as quickly as possible; the player who does not get one is out. The game continues until only one paddle is left.

140 Halt

Level 2-3   CKS

Two paddlers are back-to-back and paddle away from each other. One of the players calls 'Halt!' and they both stop and turn around on the spot. Then one of the players estimates the smallest number of strokes needed to reach the other player. The other adds his or her guess: if it is lower then the caller says 'Do it'; if not then the caller has to 'do it'. That is, the one with the lowest bid has to go to the other. If they do it in fewer strokes they win; if not, the other person wins. Alternatively, bidding takes place between two players for an agreed task. Here are some examples.

1. Spinning around on the spot three times.
2. Paddling forwards across a river to touch the bank and then returning backwards.
3. Manoeuvres in rapids.
4. A sequence of slalom gates.

The game can also be played by the whole group: players attempt an agreed task in turn, using the minimum number of strokes. The one with the least wins.

141 Greasy Pole

Level 1-2   CKS

This is a popular game on hot days, and works best with a nice old fashioned, well-rounded plastic kayak. The kayak is the greasy pole. Two players (no paddles) sit on the decks at each end facing each other, gripping the kayak with their knees, and with their feet in the water. They hold their hands on their heads and then try to unbalance their opponent, so that he or she falls into the water.   *Mel Reed*

Plas Y Brenin

KS

Sweep Strokes

142 T Bone
Level 1-2

Two boats line up nose to nose (fig 1) at the command go, they try to push their opponent around 90 degrees so they end up being T boned (fig 2). Usually best of three is the winner.

This is an excellent game as a follow up to teaching sweep strokes - it definitely lends itself to developing powerful sweep strokes.

Phil Hadley

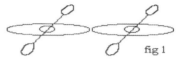

fig 1

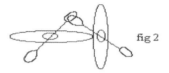

fig 2

 CKS

Stern Rubber

143 Head to Head
Level 2-3

Paddlers partner up. Then partners paddle towards each other and at the last minute each paddler puts a stern rudder in on opposite sides, but they steer so that their craft scrape past each other, side to side. Participants should be briefed to try this game slowly at first, and that care is needed to make sure that as the paddles are placed into the stern rudder position, that they do not bash their partner s head.

Lawrence Chapman

 CKS

BLINDFOLDS

144 Guide Dogs
Level 2-4

Divide the whole group into pairs. One member of the pair is blindfolded and guided by the other. They may just go for a short paddle or through an obstacle course. You could involve a slalom course, portage or even a repair. After a short time the pairs change places.

150 Tug-of-war   Level 1-4

This game is played in the same way as on dry land except that if you are using several boats in the team then many short ropes are used rather than one long rope. This is for safety reasons, as a long rope might trap players during the game. The boats are linked together by the short ropes and a rag is tied on the rope that separates the two teams.

If possible, mark out the playing area with floating markers. You will need an external judge. It's not advisable to have more than three or four on each side. It's a very good strengthening exercise for the arms! Tug-of-war is great fun and can go on for ages.

151 Sideways Tug-o-War   Level 1-4

Three boats join together as a raft, with the centre person/s holding the outside boats together strongly. The outside paddlers then try and pull the raft sideways using draw strokes and working against each other. Care needs to be taken not to hit the centre person with the paddles.

Plas Y Brenin

CKS

SHORT ROPES
Reverse Paddling,
Emergency stopping

152 Backwards Tug-o-War — Level 1-4

Connect the bow loops of two boats using a short rope (50cm is ideal). Line up the two boats and on the word GO the participants paddle backwards as hard as possible. The winner is obviously the one who pulls the opponent past a marker (the Instructor?). I find that this game works best organised as a knockout with the non-combatants lined up in their boats cheering on their chosen favourite. This is a great game for developing strong emergency stops and reverse paddling skills.

Les Stewart

 CKS

PADDED JOUSTING
RODS

153 Jousting — Level 1-3

This is a very popular game, with lots of fun to be had both for players and spectators. The idea is for one person to manoeuvre the boat whilst another person holds the jousting rod and tries to knock the other team's jouster off the boat. The jouster sits on the front deck with feet in the water—this works with kayaks, canoes and sit on tops. Alternatively, if a canoe is being used, then to make it more tippy the jouster can stand on the seat.

Design the jousting rod safely so that it is light and well padded at one end: remember it could fall apart after a few minutes of play if it is not padded adequately. Alternatively, you might simply use a paddle with lots of padding at one end.

Rules can be made up according to the ability of the group. If paddlers are new to the sport then the aim can be simply to knock the jouster off. If they are experienced, and know how to roll, then the aim can be to knock the jouster off and turn the paddler over. You must decide whether a person who has been knocked off is out, or whether they can climb back on again. (Remember, no jousting from the water!) If they climb back on then it is a good idea to impose a time limit. The game can be played in different ways:

1. As a knock-out tournament.
2. With two teams of any number.
3. With several pairs fighting one another - last one up wins.

154 Sitting Ducks (Joist) Level 1-2

Two teams line up on opposite sides of a rectangular playing area. One team have plastic ducks (or other suitable buoyant objects) sitting on their front decks. They have to make their way from one side of the area to the other running a gauntlet as the opposition try to dislodge the ducks by splashing as they pass. The number of ducks still in position on completing the crossing indicates the points scored. The opposition then take their turn.

Dave Williams

155 Throwline Surf Level 1-3

CKS

ROPE & STERN RUDDER

Attach some throw lines to the front of some of the boats in your group. Have some of your group stand on the bank holding the line. They have to pull the paddler and boat towards the shore, the paddler has to use a stern rudder to keep the boat straight. Have a Tow Master in charge of each team who directs operations and shouts commands.

Melhonie Cheseldine

Lou Monouch

CKS

156 Animal Farm

Level 1-2

The group is split into equal teams, each team will be made up of a type of animal.. The organiser will take each person in turn and give them the name of an animal, this will not be known to any of the others. The paddlers start to move in a circle, on the organiser s command they start to mimic the noise made by their animal, by locating the calls of other cows, pigs, sheep etc the paddlers come together as a team and form a raft. The first complete raft wins.

Dave Williams

CKS

BLINDFOLDS

157 Night Time Animals

Level 1-2

As above except that the paddlers are blind-folded and it is not necessary to keep each individual s animal identity from the others. The area must be well controlled and consideration given to eliminating paddles to avoid accidents.

Dave Williams

CKS

TEAM COLOURS

158 Switch

Level 1-4

This requires a way of distinguishing 2 teams, whether different coloured helmets, pegs on boats or whatever. Everyone picks someone on the opposite team and on the Go command starts to follow that person. Explain that if they find someone else is already following their chosen boat they must switch and follow someone else. After a bit of confusion you should find everyone following each other round in one or more big circles.

You can now introduce the commands "Switch" and "Reverse". On switch, you simply follow someone else. More chaos ensues until each finds a unique boat to follow. On reverse everyone must stop, then paddle backwards, following the person they find behind them (or you could get everyone to spin around and carry on following the same person).

It s a game that encourages good rear observation and back paddling.

It can be developed further with hundreds of possible commands to make it a fun game.

Phil Lyon

This needs a hoop, buoy, or some similar target about 10m off shore (or perhaps a target on the far bank). Paddlers team up in twos or threes, with one in the boat and the others on the shore. The others give the boat a big push aiming it like a dart at the buoy. The person in the boat is only allowed to use a stern rudder to steer their dart for a bulls eye on the target. Everyone has a go and gets marked for nearness to the target. The team with the best overall score wins the darts competition - and buys everyone else a round?

HOOP & BUOY
Stern Rudder,
Support Strokes

Plas Y Brenin

Plas y Brenin

DEVIANT PADDLING GAMES

The games help people think and use their body creatively. They can also add interest on a journey. These games are all different, sometimes crazy ways of paddling a boat - or getting in and out of it. Sensible, boring coaches wouldn't think of playing games like this - totally pointless they mutter - however we think they are fun and deviant. In our view you have to be a bit deviant to take up paddling - no normal sensible person is going to take up a sport that is at times so nasty, cold, wet, and involves such a loss of personal dignity!

...deviant people kayak !

DEVIANT GAMES

Game	Boat	Skill Development.	Level	Stroke	Good?
170. Doggy paddle	KCS	Balance, push/pull, co-ordination, turning, start & stop.	1-2	N/A	2
171. Paddling forwards looking backwards	KCS	As above + feel.	1-2	Various	2
172. Nose to Nose	KCS	Balance, posture, control, twisting, stretching.	1-3	Various	2
173. Object carrying	KCS	Balance, posture, control, strength development.	1-5	Various	1
174. Bucket seat	K	Balance, control.	1-3	Various	1
175. Crab seat	KC	Rotation, balance, control, push/pull.	1-3	Various	3
176. Back deck paddling	KS	Balance, active posture, control, push/pull, turning, start & stop.	1-3	Various	3
177. Back deck kneeling	KCS	Balance, active posture, bending, stretching, twisting, turning.	2-4	Various	2
178. Helicopter	KCS	Balance, bending, stretching, twisting, turning, co-ordination.	1-2	N/A	1
179. Canoe a kayak	KS	Balance, active posture, rotation, push/pull, power transfer, speed, angle, edge.	1-5	Various	3
180. Body sailing	KS	Balance, rotation, feel.	1-3	N/A	2
181. Hang ten	KCS	Balance, reaction.	1-5	N/A	2
182. Signpost	KCS	Balance, reaction.	1-3	N/A	1
183. Punting	KS	Balance, push/pull, control, turning,	1-3	N/A	3
184. Forward roll	K	Balance, control, bending, stretching, co-ordination and agility.	1-2	N/A	1
185. Rear end roll out	K	As above.	1-2	N/A	1
186. Dry feet exit	KS	Speed, balance, co-ordination, agility.	1-3	Various	3
187. Deep water solo entry	KC	Balance, stretching, bending, co-ordination, trim, edge.	2-3	N/A	3

PADDLE GRIP GAMES

Game	Boat	Skill Development.	Level	Stroke	Good?
190. Wide grip	KS	Balance, stretching, bending, co-ordination, rotation, feel through the blade.	1-3	Various	1
191. Close grip	KS	As above	1-3	Various	1
192. Cross grip	KS	As above	1-3	Various	1
193. Behind the back grip	KS	As above	1-3	Various	1
194. Crossed hands behind the back	KS	As above	1-3	Various	1
195. Over side paddling	KS	As above	1-3	Various	2
196. Crossed hands over side paddling	KS	As above	1-3	Various	1

DRY = Dry Land Game

DAMP = Afloat but should stay dry

WET = Some chance of splashing and accidental capsize

SWIM = High probability of a swim or similar

DEVIANT PADDLING

170 Doggy Paddle   Level 1-2   KCS

This game can be used as a fun way of covering a distance or as a silly race. The idea is to lie face down on the kayak. To stop the boat being too tippy players should open their legs wide apart and rest them in the water like outriggers. Hands are free to propel the boat through the water. If the paddlers can handle this they can try it with their legs out of the water on the top deck, or on their backs!

171 Paddling Forwards Looking Backwards   Level 1-2   KCS

This is a good game for covering a well-known stretch in a new and interesting way. Players hold their paddle and sit in their canoe or kayak as normal, but this time they look backwards as they paddle forwards. They must lay their head on the back deck as shown in the illustration. The game can be played on any safe stretch of water; players should paddle slowly if the space is confined. One person should supervise to avoid any accidents.

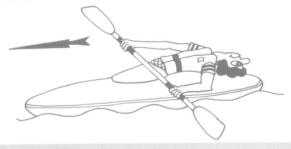

172 Nose to Nose   Level 1-3   K

The aim is for each paddler to touch their own nose to the nose of their own boat without falling in. For some people in some boats the nose dips under the water and you have to put your head under water, the thing then is to slide back up the boat without falling off!

Laurence Chapman

173 Object Carry   Level 1-5   KCS

There are many things you can add to a kayak or canoe to make paddling   SUNDRY OBJECTS
harder or funnier, or make the boat more interesting to look at.
1. Put buckets of water on the back of the boats, or tie them to the back and drag them behind in the water.
2. Make a shovel for the front of the boat (the Bulldozer).
3. Carry a change of clothes on the deck and then put them on in the boat, away from the bank.
4. Tie empty boats to the front and back of your own boat.
5. Carry a ball balanced on the front deck.

K

174 Bucket Seat
Level 1-3

This is a good confidence game and a fun way to paddle. It can be used when you are on a journey and need to stretch out (you often see photos of expedition kayakers in this pose, taking it easy on some exotic foreign river). It is not tippy, but be careful when you are getting in and out of the position — it s often best to raft up for this.

KC

175 Crab Seat
Level 1-3

This is really fun and can be used as part of a race. Swing your legs over one side of the cockpit, take the paddle, then paddle the boat sidewards. The boat becomes a very different craft. You can have the paddle in front or behind you to go forwards or backwards. You can pull the water to you or push it away You could also use different hand grips.

KS

176 Back Deck Paddling
Level 1-3

Sit on the back deck then carefully lift your legs on to the front deck and paddle. This will take a bit of practice if you are to stay upright. Once you are on the move it gets a little more stable. It's much easier to write about than do!

Plas y Brenin - www.pyb.co.uk

KCS

177 Back Deck Kneeling
Level 2-4

This is easier on the back of a canoe than of a kayak but that's no reason not to try it! Kneel on the back and paddle; remember, the boat is more stable on the move.

178 Helicopter

Level 1-2 KCS

Set your group the problem I want you to turn your boat round without touching the water or anything else . The solution is to lie back in the bucket seat position, or flat along the deck. Hold your paddle in the air with both hands and give it a twirl just like a helicopter rota—this should cool you off nicely, one way or another!

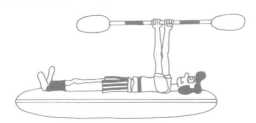

179 Canoe a Kayak

Level 1-5 KS

Sweep strokes

A difficult trick is to imitate canoe paddling by kneeling in your kayak. This is a lot tippier than being in a normal open canoe. You must be comfortable and safe - so you can fall out without scraping your legs or getting stuck. Kneeling on the seat facing the stern works well in most boats. If you have them, dragon boat paddles are really good for this game but if you don't have a canoe paddle just use one side of the kayak paddle.

You could even try a sillier version of this game by kneeling on one knee with the other foot in front, copying the sprint position. When you can paddle it well, try some more advanced strokes such as the following.

1. Backwards.
2. Draw stroke.
3. J Stroke.
4. Switching sides.
5. Cross bow.
6. Emergency stops.

180 Body Sailing

Level 1-2 KS

Sweep strokes

Try standing on the deck of your boat using your body and paddle to catch the wind. If you can manage this, then the next stage is to try to steer with the paddle by catching the wind with one blade. Good luck!

KCS

181 Hang Ten
Level 1-5

Imagine that your boat is a surf board - walk to the end and try to dangle ten toes over the end. Have a good swim!

KCS

182 SignPost
Level 1-3

You will only have a few seconds to do this, as it is so tippy. The idea is to stand on one leg in your boat with the rest of your arms and legs sticking up in the air like a signpost pointing in all directions.

KS

183 Punting
Level 1-3

This could be used in the Cambridge or Oxford areas! In a kayak, stand up just in front of the seat. Hold your paddle high up and, instead of paddling along, try to push off the bottom. You can even use a pole!

K

184 Forward Roll
Level 1-2

Get to a crouching or standing position with feet in the cockpit, then put you head on the deck in front of you and do a forward roll into the water, the kayak should stay upright.   *Laurence Chapman*

K

185 Rear End Roll Out
Level 1-2

This is another flashy way of getting out. You won't find it in any manual! Sit on the back deck, bend your legs and roll back along the deck until you meet the water.

186 Dry Feet Exit

Level 1-3 KS

Everyone has seen windsurfers coming in after a good day's surfing. They sail right up on to the beach and then just walk off their board. It can also be done in a kayak or canoe. Paddle in fast and go as far as possible up the bank. Then get out of your cockpit area, but instead of getting your feet wet, crawl along the front deck to dry land. If you are really cool you can walk along the deck.

187 Deep Water Solo Entry

Level 2-3 KC

For some unknown reason you find yourself in the water next to your boat. Now the problem is how to get back in.

In a kayak one way is to turn it over, get inside it and roll up. This results in a boat full of water, so why not try climbing up the back deck with your body as low as possible to keep it as stable as you can? Once you are lying over the cockpit area sit up fast and let your body drop into the seat. Then just put your legs in.

Plas y Brenin - www.pyb.co.uk

By changing the hand grip on the paddle shaft you bring a completely different set of muscles into action. The more adventurous the grip, the harder it becomes to steer a straight course, let alone to go fast. These grips can make for some fun races. Get everyone together, facing the same way. Tell them which grip is to be used and then shout 'Go!', upon which command they all dash to the finish line. You can vary the race in any way you want: try the following variations.

1. Race to the end, turn around and race back.
2. Race to the end and then paddle backwards using the same grip.
3. Introduce a 360¡ turn.
4. Blow a whistle during the race and call out a new grip.
5. This game can also be used on a journey if you have a dull bit.

We recommend the following grip sequences:

KS

190 Wide Grip
Level 1-3

The hand grip is moved as wide as possible so that the hands are touching the blades. This gives a feeling of the body rotating. Make sure the sides of the kayak are smooth as players hands may run along it.

KS

191 Close Grip
Level 1-3

The hands are placed close together so that they are touching. Tell the players not to let their hands creep apart half-way through the game.

192 Cross Grip

The hands are crossed on the shaft with a gap of at least 5 inches. Tell the players not to give up as it is possible with practice. If they go off-course they can try a sweep stroke.

193 Behind The Back Grip

The paddle is placed behind the back with the knuckles facing forwards. Once in this position the player tries to paddle forwards. When they think they have done well, tell them to try going fast and then change direction

194 Crossed Hands Behind The Back

This is where it starts to get silly. This is similar to the behind-the-back grip but with the added problem of having crossed hands. Players should be prepared to hit the wall so it might not be ideal for the swimming pool!

KS

195 Over Side Paddling   Level 1-3

Here the paddle is placed at the side of the boat and is used to move it sideways. The paddle is held and used as normal. This is very good for body rotation.

KS

196 Crossed Hands Over Side Paddling   Level 1-3

This is similar to over-side paddling but this time the hands are crossed. You may want to introduce a 360¡ turn in the same position.

Sue Ottoline

RAFT GAMES

These are great fun and full of variety. As many of the games involve walking, running, or crawling on the raft you should use strong, high-volume boats. Participants should be warned to mind their fingers!

Paddles are usually bunched across the cockpits and under everyone's arms, but sometimes a game may be safer with no paddles on the raft.

Many of these games are best suited to kayaks but most can be played with open canoes or sit on tops.

Many open canoes have sharper edges and more scope for minor injury than kayaks and sit on tops - so you need to take this into account before playing a game like Cat and mouse.

RAFT GAMES

Game	Boat	Skill Development.	Level	Stroke	Good?
200. Cat and Mouse	KCS	General movement skills - balance, feel, reaction, control.	1-2	N/A	
201. Alternate raft stand	KCS	As above.	1-2	N/A	
202. Mexican Wave	KCS	As above.	1-2	N/A	
203. Mass raft stand	KCS	As above.	1-2	N/A	
204. Moving raft going nowhere	KCS	As above.	1-2	N/A	
205. Stand off raft	KCS	As above.	1-2	N/A	
206. Ring Raft	KCS	As above.	1-2	N/A	
207. Raft chasing	KCS	Control, turning, speed, stop & start, accleration.	1-5	Various	
208. Kaleidoscope	KCS	Control, turning, speed, stop & start.	1-5	Various	
209. Singing raft	KCS	General movement skills - balance, feel, reaction, control.	1-2	N/A	
210. Raft wobble	KCS	Balance, feel, reaction, control, upper and lower body separation.	1-2	N/A	
211. Raft up	KCS	Balance, control, speed, co-operation, steering & sideways skills.	1-2	Various.	
212. Sinking island	KCS	General movement skills — balance, feel, reaction, control.	1-2	N/A	

DRY = Dry Land Game

DAMP = Afloat but should stay dry

WET = Some chance of splashing and accidental capsize

SWIM = High probability of a swim or similar

This must be one of the most common kayak games played anywhere in the world and most people enjoy it. All the players raft up facing the same direction with their paddles across the cockpits. Everybody in the raft holds the boat on either side of them tightly, so there are no gaps between the boats.

Give numbers to everybody. Then have a warm-up by asking one person to get out of their boat and walk, crawl, or run around the rest of the raft and return to their cockpit. After a few people have tried it you can begin the game.

Explain that you will shout out a direction and then two numbers. The first number will be the cat and the second is the mouse to be chased. On the word 'Go!' they both get out of their boats and run twice around the raft in the given direction. The idea is for the cat to touch the mouse. If the mouse is not caught by the time they have run around the raft and back into their cockpit then they win.

If it s a square raft, then players must run around the outside of the raft and pass the two outside people at either end. Cutting through the people in the middle of the raft is not allowed. You might introduce the following variations.

1. Have more than one person being chased.

2. Change direction as they run.

3. Allow players to pass anywhere between the people rafted up.

PGL Travel

201 Alternate Raft Stand   Level 1-2   CKS

Sweep strokes

Players raft up with their paddles out of the water in front. Give everybody a number. Get all the odd numbers to stand up, while the others hold the boats together tightly. After they sit down the others have a turn. When the people are standing up you can ask them to hold hands. This might also be used as part of a display. Once standing and holding hands try doing the next game -

RAFT GAMES

KCS

202 Mexican Wave
Level 1-2

When your group is rafted up get alternate people to stand up and link hands with the people either side of them. Then starting at one end you can get a Mexican wave to pass along the raft. Once this is mastered you can try it with hands raised and having to bend forwards to create the wave. On warm days, if you fancy rescue practice you could try it with the whole team standing.

 KCS

203 Mass Raft Stand
Level 1-2

Everybody rafts up, then players all stand up and hold hands. The aim is not to fall in. Another, even more difficult game would be for all players to hold hands and then try to stand up together. Very hard, but what fun trying!

 KCS

204 Moving Raft Going Nowhere
Level 1-2

This is a sillier game than the silly ones. Everybody makes a raft. There is no need for paddles. Each person holds the boat on either side of them. The aim is to move the raft forwards without touching the water or letting go of the kayak next to you. The results are a little different from what you might expect!

KCS

205 Stand Off Raft
Level 1-2

Make a standard raft. Two players have to get out of their boats and stand on the decks of two adjacent kayaks. As they stand opposite each other they look in each other's eyes, raising their arms up to shoulder height. They have to push the other off balance or to bluff them into losing their balance. Pushing is only allowed by slapping the palms of their hands. The two main techniques used are: one person pushes the other; the person pushed bends their arms to absorb the shock so that their opponent may fall. The players are not allowed to move their feet. If they move their feet or fall in, the victor scores one point, going up to a maximum of five.

RAFT GAMES

It s great fun to make a circular raft. This needs as many boats as possible at least a dozen. To form the raft, instruct everyone to hold each others boats tightly but to leave a gap between the boats at the cockpits. It helps if people lean forward (so that the fronts of the boats get pulled together) and if you have two good paddlers at each end, who paddle forwards and scull towards each other until they meet and join up. You now have a ring of boats with everyone facing inwards -very sociable, and many games can be played in this raft position.

207 Raft Chasing Level 1-5 KCS

This can be played in a raft or with the boats lined up side by side with a foot or so between them. Give each player a number. Shout out two numbers. The first is the chaser and the second is the one to be chased. Players with these numbers then break out of the raft and paddle as fast as they can twice around the raft until they return to the place they started from. The chaser has to touch any part of the other person to win. If they don't succeed, the other wins. An alternative game would be simply a race between two people. When two numbers are called the players have to race twice around the raft and the first back to their place wins. Players can go in any direction they wish.

208 Kaleidoscope Level 1-5 KCS

Draw Strokes

All boats form a loose pin-wheel with their bows to the centre, (you could use a buoy as a central point.) The object then is to perform a succession of synchronised manoeuvres - spin to left/right, reverse out, 360° rotations etc.

Dave Williams

RAFT GAMES

209 Singing Raft

This is for young children or adults being silly on a course. While people are standing up in their boats, all rafted up, preferably in a ring raft, they have to put their hands on their heads and then sing a song such as The Grand Old Duke of York' or 'Hands, shoulders, knees and toes. Another variation would be for some to stand and the rest to hold the raft together: when the singing starts the ones standing up do the actions. Another amusing variation would be for players to complete a song before they reach a particular point. This often has a strange effect on the rhythm!

www.focused-on-adventure.com

210 Raft Wobble

This is fun and popular with little children. Get them all to raft up without their paddles. Everybody holds the kayaks next to them and then starts to rock them from side to side as vigorously as possible and for as long as they are having fun.

211 Raft Up

The group paddles around in a small area. The leader shouts 'Raft up!' and a number. Players raft up in small groups of this number, as quickly as possible. Those left out and the last to raft up lose a life. The raft splits up and everyone paddles around again. This time the leader may shout out a variation, such as 'Raft up in fives facing in alternate directions!'. The game continues until only one player, the winner, remains. If you are good at maths you can arrange it so that two people win. This makes it more fun.

Here is a game in which players are guaranteed to get wet. Players raft up. The person at the end then gets out of their kayak and moves on to the rest of the raft. Meanwhile, their boat is let loose to drift off. When the person has found a stable position the next person gets on to the raft and lets their boat drift off. This game goes on until the raft or island sinks. The aim is to see how many people can stay afloat with as few boats as possible. This game needs careful supervision!

JOIN THE ADVENTURE!

With hundreds of locations nationwide there is an adventure for everyone on the water.

From starter sessions, guided tours and skills courses for the absolute beginner to personal challenges and advanced courses for the experienced paddler, you're bound to find something near you.

Discover your fun:
britishcanoeing.org.uk

PGL Travel

RACES

It is possible to write a whole book on races; the variations are endless. Most of the games in this book can be used in a race situation. Races are great fun for participants and spectators alike. Some people like to win, others just enjoy taking part. Apart from other races in the book here are some ideas for starters.

- Hand paddling

- Using objects such as table tennis bats, floats, or broom handles, instead of paddles.

- Standing up races

- Rescues

- Canoe gunwale paddling

- Carrying people

- Dipping

- Boat emptying

- Blindfolded

- Sideways paddling

- Kneeling in kayak

- Different types of boat relay

- Le Mans start (run to the boats first)

- Standing on your head drinking a milkshake while reading a magazine.

Think of something and try it.

RACES

Game	Boat	Skill Development.	Level	Stroke	Good?
220. Javelin race	KS	Power transition, push/pull, control, balance, speed, rotation.	2	Hand paddling	
221. 3, 2, 1	CKS	As above + teamwork.	2	Various	
222. Slalom obstacle course	CKS	As above + pace control and acceleration.	2-3	Various	
223. K1, K2, K3 fun sprints	KS	As above	1-4	Various	
224. Chariots	KS	As above + teamwork.	1-3	Various	
225. Catamaran	CKS	As above	1-3	Various	
226. Ski shoes	K	As above	1-3	Various	
227. Last paddler up	KS	As above	1-2	Various	
228. Koala, flying angel	CKS	Various	1	Various	
229. Macaroons	CKS	As above.	1-3	Various	
230. Back-to-back paddling	K	As above	2	Forwards & reverse.	
231. Push me pull ya	K	As above	1-3	Forwards & reverse.	
232. Water beetles	K	Power transition, push/pull, control	2	N/A	
233. Caterpillar	KS	Power transition, push/pull, control.	1-3	Various	
234. Spider boat	KS	Power transition, push/pull, control.	1-3	N/A	
235. Silly skegs	KS	Power transition, push/pull, control, active posture, speed.	1-2	Various	
236. Flip flop propulsion	KS	As above.	1-2	N/A	

DRY = Dry Land Game
DAMP = Afloat but should stay dry

WET = Some chance of splashing and accidental capsize
SWIM = High probability of a swim or similar

220 Javelin Race

Level 2   KS

Mark out a starting and a finishing line. Line up the group at one end. They then throw their paddles as far as possible towards the finish, then paddle with their hands to pick it up and throw it again until they reach the finishing line. The first over the line wins. Make sure there is plenty of space between the paddlers so they do not get hit by stray paddles.

RACES

Lou Manouch

221 Three, Two, One

Level 2   C

MARKERS

This requires two or more teams of about five people. Set a course approximately 50m long, with marker buoys or markers along the bank. Teams race to the first marker and then must abandon one boat. The paddler from that boat then has to be carried by one of the other boats in the team. The race continues to the next marker and every time the team reaches a marker another boat has to be abandoned. This continues until everybody is carried by one boat. First over the line wins.

222 Slalom Obstacle Course   Level 2-3

This is a fun slalom event. You put up some gates with obstacles in between. You might use some of the following obstacles.

- Ladder slide.
- Limbo.
- Log jump.
- Paddle through the tyre or large hoop.
- Zig-zag, between poles in the mud.
- Thread the eye of the needle between two poles/buoys (squeeze through without touching.
- Over an over-turned kayak.
- Throwing a ball into a bucket
- It could be either just a fun paddle, or you could time each paddler and count penalties.
- Why not try a team event with ten in each team?

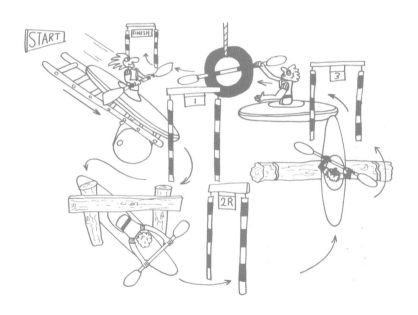

 K

223 K1, K2 & K3 Fun Sprints   Level 1-4

Make up a course. It could be straight, or have bends or obstacles. In each class the players, one two or three to a boat, sit on the deck with their legs outside the cockpit area. Line up the boats for a mass start. On the word 'Go!' they race to the finishing line. The first boat wins. Note that this game is safer played with floats or hands as paddles.

There are many variations of chariot races but the principles are the same: two people in kayaks raft up to each other facing in the same direction, with a paddle each for propulsion. The idea is to paddle along and carry others on the back decks. A variation is for one person to put a paddle across the kayaks just behind the cockpit and sit on it with their feet in each kayak. The other person stands up with a foot in each of the kayaks and uses a paddle to move them both forwards,

Plas y Brenin - www.pyb.co.uk

225 Catamaran   Level 1-3   CKS

This game requires two people and two kayaks. The idea is for both to share the two kayaks and to paddle forwards. Each paddler has to sit outside the cockpit with one foot in each boat. Remember, never have more than one person inside the same kayak. There are two variations on this game: the first is for the paddlers to face each other; and the second is for the paddlers to sit next to each other. Paddles can be used for propulsion.

K

226 Ski Shoes
Level 1-3

For this game you will need two kayaks, one paddle and one player. The idea is for a player to wear one kayak on each foot and then stand up and paddle forwards over a given distance. The two kayaks are placed side by side facing the same direction, and the paddler places one foot in the cockpit of each kayak..

Plas y Brenin - www.pyb.co.uk

K

227 Last Paddler Up
Level 1-2

Form teams of three, rafted up on a start line and facing a marker buoy or boat. On the word 'Go!' one person from each team paddles around the marker and returns to a position between their two team-mates who raft up and support the centre boat. The middle paddler stands up straight and then sits down again. The sequence is then repeated until all three team members have had a go.

228 Koala, Flying Angel

Level 1   C

The illustrations show three ways of carrying small children. They can be used for fun rides, races, or for learning rescue techniques. Canoes are more suitable for these types of games as they are wider and more stable. Care must be taken that the paddles do not jam the child's hands or feet. For kayaks, remember the rule that only one person is allowed in the cockpit — so in other words the child s legs must be outside, and of course both must wear buoyancy aids.

229 Macaroons

Level 1-3   CK

This requires two teams, one made up of experienced paddlers, the other of inexperienced paddlers. The new paddlers paddle to the nearest bank, leave their boats to drift, and run all the way around to the other side of the lake where the good paddlers have gone. The runners get on to a raft made by the good paddlers and are taken to their drifting boats. The game is over when all are in the boats.

230 Back-to-Back Paddling   Level 2

Here is a tricky one, as it is an unnatural and very tippy way of paddling. Two people sit on one kayak, back-to-back with their feet in the water. They have to share one paddle which is between their backs. They hold the paddle with both hands and their knuckles facing forwards. On the word 'Go!' paddlers try to paddle to a mark in front of them. The boat who makes it first wins.

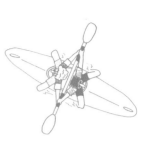

231 Push Me Pull Ya   Level 1-3

In this game you will need teams of two players with one kayak; both players have paddles. The two paddlers sit facing each other on the deck of the kayak, one on the front and the other on the back. Teams line up and on the word 'Go!' a race commences. The paddlers at each end always paddle in different directions - i.e. the one who is facing forwards paddles forwards and the one facing backwards paddles backwards. The kayak should move forwards. There is no need to turn around at the end, as players simply change the direction in which they are paddling.

232 Water Beetles.   Level 2

Everyone lines up on the start-line ready to race to a given finishing point. On the command 'Get ready!' they lift their legs out of their kayak and let them dangle in the water on either side. Then they lie forwards, opening their legs for support. On the word 'Go!' they use their legs and arms as fast as they can to get to the finishing line without turning over. If they fall off they must climb back on in the same spot before continuing. Before the start you must decide whether players are allowed to grab hold of other players' legs to move forwards, and whether pushing is allowed.

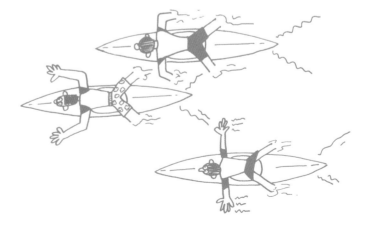

233 Caterpillar

Level 1-3   KS

This game requires teams of three. One person is properly seated in the kayak; they can use either a paddle or their hands. The other two people lie on the front and back decks of the kayak, as in the 'Spider boat' below. The two on the decks do not use paddles. If the person in the kayak uses a paddle they must be careful not to hurt their passengers' hands.

234 Spider Boat

Level 1-3   KS

This is a team game, two people per team. One member lies straddled on the back deck with their arms and legs out- stretched in the water for support. The other member lies straddled on the front deck facing the opposite way, so that their heads are close together above the cockpit area, as shown in the illustration. A variation is for both paddlers to face the same way.

235 Silly Skegs

Level 1-2   K

ALTERNATIVE SKEGS

A skeg helps a paddler to go straight in their kayak. Why not make some silly skegs. or put the proper ones on the wrong way so the boat will not go in a straight line? Players line up and race to a given point. Do not let paddlers practise before-hand. Try a helmet, a throw line, a towline, or a paddle.

236 Flip Flop Propulsion

Level 1-2   KS

FLIP FLOPS

This is called Thongs propulsion' if you are Australian.
Great fun for a race, but make sure that the footwear floats first! If you have a really expert group then you could ask people to try a roll.

RACES

Plas Y Brenin

RESCUE GAMES

Rescues seem to be for the very serious people with big buoyancy aids and giant throwlines. Those kind of people think it would be a crime if we were to make the teaching and training of rescues fun, and for that reason you must not smile at all when learning to throw a line at your swimming buddy or be anything other than very Ernest! (Ernest was a particularly serious rescuer that we used to know.)

Alternatively, you could simply view rescue skills as the ones you're probably going to need if you play all the other games in this book!

We personally feel that the games to learn these skills are equally as valid as that paddle waggling stuff - so here are a few games which are pretty wet and only to be done with a serious look on your face, furrowed eye brows and a steely glint in your eye!

RESCUE GAMES

Game	Boat	Skill Development.	Level	Stroke	Good?
240. Inner-tube tow	CKS	Power transfer, dynamic posture, rotation, edge, trim, gliding, sliding.	1-3	Forward	
241. Towing Competitions	CKS	Power transfer, active posture, rotation, lean, balance.	1-3	Forward	
242. Towing tag	KS	As above	1-3	Forward	
243. One-person rescue	KS	As above	1-3	Forward	
244. Patient carry	CKS	As above	1-3	Various	
245. Bertie the Tug Boat	KS	As above	1-3	Forward	
246. Mass towing game	KS	As above	1-3	Forward	
247. Sticks	CKS	Reaction, anticipation, spatial awareness, speed, position, co-ordination.	2-5	N/A	
248. Hear no Evil	CKS	Communication, body language, sense of urgency.	2-4	N/A	
249. Raft Repair	CKS	Various	1-3	N/A	
250. All Out	CKS	Balance, communication, teamwork.	1-3	N/A	

DRY = Dry Land Game

DAMP = Afloat but should stay dry

WET = Some chance of splashing and accidental capsize

SWIM = High probability of a swim or similar

..and if he doesn't need a rescue by the time I get there, he sure will when I've finished with him!....

Foxy©

240 Inner-Tube Tow

Level 1-3   CKS

This is a simple towing game which could be used by several teams in a
INNER TUBE
fun race. Basically all you have is an inner-tube attached to a canoe or a
kayak. One person sits in the inner tube and is towed by the boat. After
a while the crew change places. This is really nice on a hot day.

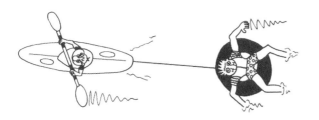

241 Towing Competitions

Level 1-3   KS

To find the most effective techniques try a competition between them -
one type verses another .- towing in line, fanned tows, short tows, long
tows, etc.   *Loel Collins*

242 Towing Tag

Level 1-3   KS

The person or boat who is It tags a boat and then has to tow that boat
to a set point before tagging and collecting more. This works well in a
small area and with a small group.   *Loel Collins*

243 One-person Rescue

Level 1-3   KS

This game is based on a rescue technique and works great as a race.
Everyone finds a partner and rafts up with their kayaks alongside each
other in their pairs, but facing each other. One plays the part of the
rescuer and the other plays the part of the one who is in need of help.
The person being rescued lays their paddle across the decks of the two
kayaks and leans across the deck of the rescuer s boat with one hand
holding the bow, and one the other side of the front deck. The job of the
victim is to clamp their kayak firmly and comfortably in place parallel to
the rescuer s kayak.
The rescuer then paddles off with the victim s boat backwards, alongside,
and slightly ahead of his. At the end of a set distance they change roles -
not places, then they come back the same way. The first pair back wins.
After the game you can tell players how the technique is used in an
emergency situation.

Peter Knowles

 CKS

244 Patient Carry
Level 1-3

There are dozens of different races involving people being rescued. You can use any sort of rescue to carry the person or persons in any state they may pretend to be (dead, broken leg, broken arm or back problems). To carry the patient/s one kayak, two kayaks, or a raft can be used. The patient might be towed in the water or lie in an open canoe. The game can also be played in relay form with people either side of the lake or river. All sorts of things could be introduced.

1. Three paddlers, one of whom gets seasick, dies or breaks a bone.

2. Two paddlers, one of whom has lost their paddle.

3. Three paddlers, one holes his boat so badly it can't be repaired. The more real you make the situation, the better the exercise!

Loel Collins

245 Bertie The Tug Boat

Level 1-3 KS

In this rescue-type game there are two kayaks stranded with only one person to rescue them. The rescuer gets the two stranded kayakers to raft up side by side facing in the same direction. The rescuer moves in between them at the front (facing them). The aim is to push them over a given distance. First back are the winners. Then the paddlers can change around so that everyone gets a turn.

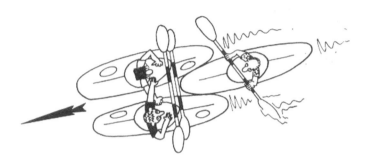

246 Mass Towing Game

Level 1-3 KS

This is the same as the double towing game, but this time you have six to ten kayaks rafted up to one rescuer. With a large group like this you can introduce more rescuers to push the raft along.

247 Sticks

Level 2-5 CKS

One of the biggest problems people have when throwing a rescue line to someone swimming in a river, is learning to accommodate the speed of the water into the throw. Throw a log into the river, allow it to float past the group. The group throw stones at the log to try to hit it and this gives them practice at how much to allow for the speed of the current. It also encourages an over-arm throwing action. Be careful who you play this game with - just to make sure they are not going to break someone s windows!

Loel Collins

RESCUE GAMES

248 Hear No Evil

Level 2-5

Getting people to use rescues that are simple and low risk can be difficult! Talking/shouting rescues are the least risk and give best results. So split your group into 2 halves, half the group are the rescuers who stand in a circle. The other half are the victims, who are brought one by one, into the centre of the circle with their eyes shut. The rescuers(people on the outside of the circle) have to attract the blindfold victim. The victim goes to the one recuer who has attracted their attention best. The winner is the rescuer who can attract and rescue most victims.

After the first game, you can discuss what worked well and why! The groups switch and this time the rescuers cant shout they can only use body language and then you can again review what works best. Then try combining the two pick a couple of people with a mixture of positive body and actual language, and negative body and actual language.

> A. with positive body/positive actual
> B. with positive body/negative actual
> C. with negative body/positive actual
> D. with negative body/negative actual

You will normally find that Positive body will get the best results.

Loel Collins

MARKER PEN &
REPAIR TAPE

249 Raft Repair

Level 1-3

This is a useful exercise. Before you go off on a paddle, secretly put a few felt-tip marks around the boats. Then paddle out a long way from land with the group, having told one or two people to pretend that holes are letting in water and need to be repaired. The group has to make a raft and find the holes. They do this by bringing the boat up on the raft, out of the water and taping the hole. The hole can be any shape and size that your evil mind wants!

250 All Out

Level 2-5

This might be called 'All-out' or 'Wipe-out'. It is often used on Coaching courses. Everyone paddles out into part of the water that is deep and away from any physical support. On the word 'Go!' everyone turns over, including the instructor. On the next words 'It's ruddy cold' players help one another to empty the boats out and get back into them. It is often easier to start emptying the first boat by using a boat as a base to see-saw the water out. Everyone then holds the empty boat steady so the person can climb in. If you have a large group you could divide them into teams and hold a race.

3 LAKES CHALLENGE

43 PADDLING MILES | 3 COUNTRIES

BRITISH CANOEIN

LLYN TEGID (WALES - 7 M

WINDERMERE (ENGLAND - 11 M

LOCH AWE (SCOTLAND - 25 M

43 PADDLING MILES

THE 3 LONGEST LAKES IN ENGLAND, SCOTLAND AND WALES

ARE YOU READY FOR THE CHALLENGE?!

The distance completed both on and off the water and the planning involved makes the Three Lakes Challenge:

THE ULTIMATE UK PADDLING ADVENTURE!

Take on the lakes at any time and in any order, discover more at: www.britishcanoeing.org.uk

GO Canoei

   CanoeWales SCA

JOURNEY GAMES

For me kayaking and canoeing is all about exploring - a large part of that is about travelling on rivers, lakes, sea and surf. On some journeys it is simply the beauty of the surroundings that excites me and on others it s the physical challenge - I guess it all depends on your perspective.

For some of us, being outside in spaces of nature is satisfaction enough, but for some it is boring. There is nothing to do and not a Play station in sight. At first it may seem as if there is not much around you that you can use. But take another look, and you may find that the number of things to do is in fact endless: land, water,

sky, wind, trees, rocks, light, dark, snow and ice, all are waiting to be a part of an exciting adventure. If the wind blows, catch it in a sail; if there is a rock sticking out of the water, see how many of you can get out of your canoes and stand on it.

What you see during the day becomes a new adventure in the dark as you silently creep around the water's edge trying not to be seen by anybody on the land.

Work with the weather and your surroundings, not against them; use whatever conditions you have and discover how many ways the environment can be enjoyed.

JOURNEY GAMES

Game	Boat	Skill Development.	Level	Stroke	Good?
260. Walk in	CKS	Active posture, bending, lifting, agility.	1-3	N/A	
261. Jungle chain walk in	CKS	As above, pace judgement + cooperation.	1-3	N/A	
262. Follow my leader	CKS	Control, turning, speed, balance, agility.	1-5	Various	
263. Amazon river journey	CKS	Various.	1-3	Various	
264. Duck Hunting	CKS	Sliding, gliding, speed, control.	1-4	Indian stroke, slicing and feathering.	
265. Sheepdog	CKS	Speech, agility, pace and judgement.	1-3	Various	
266. Mud sliding	CKS	Turning, rotation, balance, bracing, sliding, gliding.	1-2	Various	
267. Torch light procession	CKS	Co-ordination, control, balance, awareness.	1-3	Various	
268. Scavenging and hunting	CKS	Control, turning, speed, balance, agility.	1-4	N/A	
269. Gutter Creek	CKS	Control, speed.	1-3	Various	
270. Hold that spot!	CKS	Control, speed, feel.	3-4	Various	
271. Greenpeace clear-up	CKS	Control, planning, preparation.	2-4	Various	
272. Nature awareness trail	n/a	Environmental awareness	1-5	N/A	
273. Who is teaching who?	n/a	Environmental awareness	1-5	N/A	
274. Orienteering	CKS	Control, planning, preparation.	2-4	Various	
275. Hunt the Keys	CKS	Control, planning, improvisation.	1-5	N/A	

DRY = Dry Land Game

DAMP = Afloat but should stay dry

WET = Some chance of splashing and accidental capsize

SWIM = High probability of a swim or similar

PGL Travel

260 Walk In
Level 1-3   CKS

This game starts from the car park. Instead of walking along that nice, straight tarmac path to the water's edge, why not make the task a little more difficult? Find another route to the river that just happens to go through the trees and over the fence - more like the route encountered on big expeditions. They will enjoy the paddle all the more - especially if they've had to negotiate stinging nettles! Do not invade private property or damage fences.

261 Jungle Chain Walk In
Level 1-3   CKS

The idea is the same as in 'Walk in', but instead of individuals holding their own boat, players make a chain by holding one end of their craft and one end of another's. The person at the end holds the back of the boat in front of them and carries their own boat.

262 Follow My Leader
Level 1-5   CS

The object of this game is for players to follow the leader fairly closely, one behind the other. The leader chooses the course. This game may be used to cover a distance along a lake, river or canal. Variations include the following.

1. Add 360¡ turns on the spot.

2. Paddle backwards.

3. Break in and out.

4. Ferry glides.

5. Use a slalom course.

6. The leader gets out of his boat and carries it over an obstacle; he then seal launches back into the water.

7. Turn it into a race with the leader trying to open the gap between people by paddling fast or choosing a difficult route.

8. The leader rolls or capsizes (warm days only!).

CKS

263 Amazon River Journey

Level 1-3

The next time you are paddling up one of those small streams covered with weed and rushes with some young children, tell them about the Amazon and all the animals that live there. Then the group imitates the noise of the animals.

PGL Travel

CKS

Silent Paddling Skills

264 Duck Hunting

Level 1-4

Try to sneak up to whatever available (or imaginary) wildlife is around - so try to paddle completely silently. You can use a normal paddle technique or paddle with a sliced blade.   *Caroline Gerritsen*

265 Sheepdog

Level 1-3 CKS

This is a game that solves the problem of being on a journey with both fast and slow paddlers. Line up the fast paddlers at the front. Place a good helper at the back as a marker. The whole group keeps moving forwards. On the word 'Go!' the fast ones have to paddle around the marker and then back to the front. Vary the game by shouting out different instructions, such as 'Six times around!', or changing the hand grips on the paddle. In theory they should get a little tired and may even progress forwards at the same time as the others!

266 Mud Sliding

Level 1-2 KS

My mother in law would call this a nasty horrid game , and of course it has to be great fun. You find mud banks around the tidal estuaries such as the Thames or the Severn. The group paddles to the mud banks at low tide. They then line up in their boats and race to the top. This is easier said than done. Players need to take a run up to the bank and then dig their paddles into the mud to pull them selves up. It is possible with a lot of hard work and good technique to get up even really steep slopes. Players shouldn't give up if they slide back down a few times. Stick in - that is the motto!

Coming down again makes it all worthwhile. In a kayak, if you do a few sweep strokes you can spin really fast all the way down until you hit the water at high speed. If you do it properly you should be feeling very sick at the bottom. Then you can go back and do it all again!

267 Torch Light Procession

Level 1-3 CKS

This is a very pretty sight for spectators and a lot of fun for paddlers. Choose a river or canal running through a town with a few bridges for spectators. The idea is for the group to illuminate their boats and perform a torchlit procession, perhaps as part of a firework display? Bright green glow sticks work well fixed to paddles and helmets, as do head torches or flash lights inside the fronts and backs of kayaks and glowing through the plastic. How about Chinese lanterns suspended from fishing rods on canoes? It would be tempting, but irresponsible to mount a red distress flare on the back of your boat!

TORCHES

CKS

268 Scavenging & Hunting   Level 1-4

The group is paddling along the water when you stop them and tell everybody to rush into the forest, hostel or camp site on the word 'Go!' and collect a set number of objects. If it is a forest the objects could be natural things such as leaves. twigs or even beetles. You might arrange a clean-up in which the group has to collect unnatural things such as old cans and litter. If it is the hostel or camp site they might have to get more personal items like a toothbrush or a soap dish. When players have got the objects they have to rush back to their boats with them and paddle back to you. If they collect toothbrushes (their own!), you can make it more fun by making everybody clean their teeth with the toothbrush and paste as they are returning. What about giving everybody a matchbox in which to collect as many insects as possible? (Let them out afterwards!)

CKS

269 Gutter Creek   Level 1-3

If you happen to be paddling down a back stream and the paddlers are taking their time, tell the group that the stream they are paddling in, or by, is called 'gutter creek' because all the local sewers dump all their untreated waste into the stream. Watch how fast they move to get home!

CKS

270 Hold That Spot   Level 3-4

This is a game for a river with a slow moving current. Hold that Spot is the order for all paddlers to stop moving up the river and to hold their position; this means they have to paddle at the same speed as the oncoming current. Then they move again and you repeat the game further up the river. You could also try it with players going up the river backwards.

Your mission is to clean the last dump of nuclear waste so the world is rid LOTS OF GEAR
of it. Each team is given a map outlining routes and the places where the
waste is dumped. Each team is also given a survival kit comprising: one
broom stick handle; one ball of string; an old sheet off the bed, or old rain
coat.

A few hours before the event the instructor goes around the lake and
hides objects such as: a couple of tins full of a green liquid suspended
from a tree - this liquid is not allowed to touch the ground at any time in
the game or it will blow up (this is the plutonic waste); six empty old rusty
cans which are the detonators; Smarties' tops - these are de-radiation
tablets.

Draw up a set of rules like the following -

1. Plutonic waste must be picked up first.

2. Players are not allowed to touch it with their hands or any other part of
   the body.

3. Plutonic waste cannot be put down on the ground or on a boat.

4. All objects are to be picked up and carried in the order specified.

5. The survival kit can be used to make progress. (For example, use
   paddles and a sheet to make a sail.)

The game can be as complicated or as simple as you choose to make it.
Try to make use of the environment and weather conditions. Most of all,
the world must be free of nuclear waste.

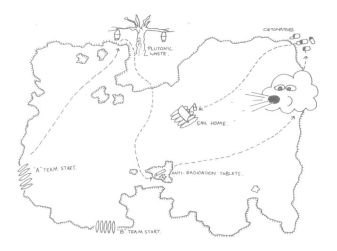

272 Nature Awareness Trail

Level 1-5

PRIOR SET UP

Since you are out in the open you should take advantage of the massive variation of wildlife. See if you can set up an aquatic nature trail with the aim of pointing out some of the interesting aspects of your area. This might be part of a school project in biology or geography. Rather than talking or reading about the subjects people can paddle along in a boat, be amongst them, learning all the time.

273 Who Is Teaching Who?

Level 1-5

IDENTIFICATION CARDS OR BOOKS

All good coaches know that we remember just 5% of what we hear, 10% of what we read and 75% of what we do (note that most of this book is about doing rather than listening!), however if we teach someone else we will recall a massive 90%. So rather than just telling your group about all the fascinating biodiversity of the environment around them, dish out a few identification carts and wildlife books and get them to look up one thing each that they can then teach the rest of the group about. Learning to look things up for themselves will help to make them independent and you may even learn something yourself. In the UK the Collins Gem books to: birds, seashore, pond life etc. are particularly good.   *Karl Midlane*

274 Orienteering

Level 2-4   CKS

This takes a bit of preparation and organisation, but is ideal for a centre with access to lots of waterways, lakes, channels, and islands. Divide the group into two teams of three or more. Each is given a map. divided into grids, of a defined area of water and the surrounding banks. Draw up a list of separate instructions guiding players to specific points at which various letters are hung from trees or rocks. Each time a team reaches a destination they find their letter and new instructions as to where the next one is. The first team back with a full set of letters. arranged to spell a given word, wins. You might use a compass depending on the age and ability of the players.

275 Hunt The Keys

Level 1-5   CKS

This is a traditional game associated with canoe and kayak journeys and although not that popular, it is still quite commonly played. Hunt the car keys is excellent for practice of patience, aggression control, and general improvisation skills. There are many versions of the game, too numerous to describe here (most coaches will have their own favourites), but caution should be used on the more extreme versions which may require survival skills.   *Mark Nichols*

Lou Manouch

CANOE GAMES

CANOE GAMES

Game	Boat	Skill Development.	Level	Stroke	Good?
300. Tandem skills	C	Dynamic posture, communication, co-ordination, co-operation, rotation, edge, trim, balance, awareness, working together	1-3	Various	
301. Balance games	C	As above	1-3	Various	
302. Wet Twister	C	As above, stretching and twisting.	1-3	Various	
303. Trim games	C	As above	1-3	Various	
304. Gunwale bobbing	C	Balance, active posture, co-ordination, feel, trim, edge, angle.	1-3	N/A	
305. Gunwale standing	C	As above	1-3	N/A	
306. Canoe Ballet	C	As 300 above + timing.	1-3	Various	
307. Exchange Stations	C	As above	1-3	Various	
308. Canoe Basket Ball	C	As above	1-3	Various	
309. Tandem Crew Lottery	C	As above	1-3	Tandem crew skills	
310. Canoe ledge climb	C	Balance, co-ordination, feel, speed, timing, push/pull, stability.	1-3	Various	
311. Hunker Hawser	C	Push pull, power transfer.	1-3	Various	

RAFTED CANOE GAMES

Game	Boat	Skill Development.	Level	Stroke	Good?
315. Ring rafts	C	Balance, posture, rotation, bending, co-ordination, leaning, stretching, working together.	1-3	N/A	
316. Fruit Salad	C	As above	1-3	N/A	
317. Pyramids	C	As above	1-3	N/A	
318. Wobbly rafts	C	As above	1-3	Various	
319. Razor Shell	C	As above	1-3	Various	
320. Raft Building	C	As above + improvisation	1-3	Various	
321. Walking the plank	C	As above	1-3	Various	
322. Raft Sailing	C	As above + feel.	1-3	Various	
323. Water World	C	As above	1-3	Various	

DRY = Dry Land Game

DAMP = Afloat but should stay dry

WET = Some chance of splashing and accidental capsize

SWIM = High probability of a swim or similar

300 Tandem Skills

Level 1-3 C

Team work is vital in a good tandem crew - get your crews to try some of the following:

1. Move off the seats into the middle of the boat.
2. Paddle facing each other in the middle of the boat or at the ends.
3. Paddle back to back in the middle of the boat or at the ends.
4. Paddle together but by only whispering.
5. Paddle with one member of the team with eyes shut.
6. With one standing.
7. Both standing.
8. One holding the tops of the paddles and one the bottom.
9. Try swapping ends.
10. Both standing.
11. One standing and jumping with the other bracing.
12. One trying a head stand with one bracing.
13. One jumping and spinning around whilst the other one braces.

I m sure you get the idea! Anything that encourages communication, co-operation, co-ordination and confidence in each other is good and great fun.

Lou Manouch

CANOE GAMES

BALL

C

301 Balance Games
Level 1-3

Try some of the following -

1. Have your tandem crew face each other across the boat at its mid point, by coordinating their efforts they can try to lean back, together but on opposite sides without capsizing the boat.

2. Have your crew reach further out with their paddles until their heads and their bodies are outside the gunwale.

3. Try both or just one standing with their feet apart gently moving their weight from foot to foot to try and create waves without falling in.

4. Put a ball in the bottom of the boat and the tandem crew have to roll the ball from side to side.

5. Have both paddlers stand up, face each other and they have to mirror each others actions. This is good fun if you can get them standing face to face, hand on hand.

Loel Collins

Lou Manouch

CARDS & DIAL

C

302 Wet Twister.
Level 1-3

On sunny warm days how about trying Wet Twister! This is the same game as the dry land warm up game — number 21 but played in the canoe out in deep water - people will get wet and/or develop balance. It also gets people used to moving around in the boat!

Loel Collins

On windy days, get your crews to try moving their position in the canoe forwards and backwards. The canoe will seem to move in the wind. Then see if the boat can be spun 360 degrees or flicked 180 degrees. Ask the crews to try moving their weight to the end of the boats to get it to wheelie and spin, - watch out the boat gets tippy the closer you get towards the end. Put a ball in the bottom of the boat and set the crews the task to get the ball to roll up and down the boat.

BALL

Loel Collins

Lou Manouch

This is precisely what the title suggests. The idea is for one person to stand with one foot on either side of the gunwale, on the end of boat and to move the canoe by bobbing it up and down. See who can stand on the furthest end of the canoe, or do the most spectacular bobs, or try a race downwind.

305 Gunwale Standing — Level 1-3

Start off with one person standing on the gunwales and then add players one by one. See how many people can do it at the same time without falling in.

306 Canoe Ballet — Level 1-3

Each tandem pair is given a choreographed routine to prepare. I suggest 4 forward strokes followed by a forward sweep (bow paddler) and reverse (stern paddler) to turn 360¡ as a pirouette; then four reverse strokes followed by a reverse pirouette.

Tandem pairs are then paired up (4 paddlers/2 boats) and must perform their routine in synchrony. If groups are really synchronised, these manoeuvres can be performed in a group or a chorus line even!

Liz Beard

307 Exchange Stations Race — Level 1-3

The teams start this race Le-Mans style; run to their boats, launch and paddle around a buoy or object. On the return leg the crew have to swap places so all members occupy a different position before arriving home.

308 Canoe Basket Ball — Level 1-3

Divide your boats into equal teams and brief them on the playing area and the rules. Each team has a ball which they try to throw into another team s boat to score a goal. A ball may be batted away by using a paddle, but may not be prevented from entering a boat by any other means. A traditional variation is that when the ball successfully lands inside a boat, a member of that crew has to jump overboard and swim ashore.

Dave Williams

Lou Manouch

309 Tandem Crew Lottery

Level 1-3   C

This is a game for when everybody has learnt a few strokes - 6 different strokes works best. This game is great to get people to understand how the strokes can be combined to achieve different things. You ll need some waterproof paper and a pencil and a dice. Bow paddler and stern paddler make a list 1-6 of the strokes they can do - for example:

PAPER, PENCIL & DICE
Tandem Crew Skills

Bow Paddler:
1. Forward Power
2. Nothing
3. Forward sweep
4. Reverse sweep
5. Reverse power
6. Bow rudder

Stern Paddler:
1. Forward Power with J stroke
2. Nothing
3. forward power without J
4. Reverse sweep
5. Reverse power
6. Stern rudder

In turn the paddlers throw a dice in the floor of the boat, if it come up 6 for the bow and then 2 for the stern, the bow does a bow rudder and the stern nothing and they can see what it does. They can keep playing until they ve sussed out what combination do what to the boat.
Once they have played the game set a small circuit, then get them to decide what combination of strokes achieves the best results.

Loel Collins

310 Canoe Ledge Climb

Level 1-3   C

Can you make a canoe climb onto a ledge? - this may sound impossible but it can be done.   One person paddles a strong canoe towards a ledge or bank (up to two foot high), then stands on the back of the canoe and gets the canoe bobbing as it approaches the ledge. The last bob should leave the front of the canoe on the ledge.   The paddler then nonchalantly walks up the front of boat and on to dry land. This is the opposite to a seal launch.

311 Hunker Hawser

Level 1-3   C

This is based on an American outdoor game. It uses two C2s or K2s. The two canoes face each other with about 6 feet between them. The person in the back of each canoe has a paddle to keep control. The person in the front of each canoe holds one end of a piece of rope about 10 feet long. The aim is to pull the other person into the water. Many tactics can be used.

ROPE

RAFTED CANOE GAMES

Rafted canoes provide a solid platform for many fun games. You can raft canoes up, just like kayaks and many of the games listed in the main Raft games chapter can be played with open canoes with certain adaptions. Open canoes often have relatively sharp edges, so do warn crews to watch that their fingers so they don t get crushed on the gunwales. With canoes, people are often safer forming a raft by everybody holding hands. Quite a good unit for raft games is 3 open canoes rafted together, with the two crew in the central boat holding onto the outside canoes, - the 4 people in the outside canoes are then free to manoeuvre the raft or play games. Then change crews round after a bit.

Loe Manouch

315 Ring Rafts   Level 1-3

With large groups you can simply attach the bows of all the boats, to form a big star shaped circle of canoes. It is safer but less secure to just have the stern paddlers holding hands to make a circular raft—this then leaves the bow paddlers free to play games!

316 Fruit Salad   Level 1-3

Raft up your tandem pairs of open canoes. Give each paddler the name of a fruit ie. apple, pear, orange, banana. On your command — all the oranges must stand and change places, then the apples, pears and bananas in turn When/if you decide to say fruit salad - everyone must change places with someone else!

Liz Beard

317 Pyramids

Level 1-3 C

Bring three canoes along side each other. Make sure these are held together and bring more canoes in, one at a time, and have the crew step in the three rafted boats. Spin the empty boat, lift and slide it up and out so that it is sitting crosswise across the three rafted canoes. Then have the crew get back in. Do the same with a second boat. If this works have a third boat arrive and place it across and on top of these two 2 boats to form a pyramid, 3,2,1.

318 Wobbly Rafts

Level 1-3 C

Have boats pair up, then the two boats come along side each other. The crew of boat A balance their boat whilst the crew of boat B step into the middle of boat A. Crew B then pull the empty boat B across and over the centre of the boat they are standing in (boat A) so that it balances out of the water, crew B then carefully get back into the boat and work their way to the ends. The team in the bottom boat A now paddle gently forwards and the top crew B try to steer and turn the raft by dipping one or other end of their boat into the water.   Eventually the top boat will slide off so it is important that everyone is warned to keep their finger clear, the lower boat sometimes capsizes when this happen but rarely the top boat.

Peter Knowles

319 Razor Shell

Level 1-3

Bring two canoes together, using a painter to tie the central thwarts tight together. Have one person sit on the knot and hold the outside gunwales of the two boats. The remaining three paddlers can now carefully stand up and place a foot in each boat to paddle.

Sweep strokes

320 Raft Building

Level 1-3

Building a raft out of several canoes is a great project, but note that it should be seen as a game and not a safety technique. Deciding to tie canoes together to make a more stable and useful raft is a difficult decision - rafted canoes can and do sink and then become virtually unmanageable. We suggest that you should make this call based on the ability of the group, and not on the conditions, i.e if you feel you need to build araft because the conditions are too rough then you really shouldn t be out there.

Here s some ideas and tips to take note of -

1. When making a raft , always have the bow of the raft slightly closer together than the stern, this reduces the build up of a wave between the boats.

2. The boats MUST be fitted with **flotation**

3. The method of construction of the raft **must be releasable**, - one of the best ways is Gazspar s - See boxed text.

4. Always leave one canoe out of the raft so you will have a boat to rescue from if required.

Simply paddling the raft around becomes a great teamwork game that requires coordination and cooperation. On warm calm days the raft becomes a platform for all kinds of wet games such as the ones below.

Loel Collins

PLANK

321 Walking The Plank

Level 1-3

Build a raft - but this, time add a plank Gadzooks! For what nefarious purpose?
Loel Collins

Karl Midlane

A nice simple piece of equipment that makes building rafts easy is a Gazspar (Gaz invented it). Take an 8 foot length of 2 by 4 timber and 2 lengths of 8-10mm bungee. Drill a hole at the end of the spar(about 6 inches in) thread the bungee through tie an overhand knot in the bungee and pull it tight. Roughly measure the width of your canoes towards the centre of the spar and drill a second hole 2 inches in from the side of the spar, cut a small notch from the side into the whole so the bungy can be pull tight and slotted into the notch. To create a raft bring the boats along side each other place the gazpar across both boats, take the bungee tight around the spar and thwart securing it tight into the notch. Do this in the central thwart and the stern thwart and you have a raft that is releasable. *Loel Collins*

322 Raft Sailing

Level 1-3   C

GAZPARS & SAIL

The raft becomes a great way of heading down wind. Here are some simple methods of using the wind for propulsion. They can be used for fun or to give you a rest while keeping on the move, as long as the wind is in the right direction. All that is needed is an old sheet and some nylon string, or an old umbrella!

1. Raft up and put your paddles in the air. The paddle is the sail.
2. Everybody rafts up facing the same way. The two people at each end take a sheet and tie it to their paddles, which they then raise in the air. It is possible for a person in the middle of the raft to use their paddle as a rudder at the rear of the raft. This will allow some steering downwind.
3. Raft two canoes, use a third canoe (on its side) as a sail.
4. Umbrella sailing. What can I say, but to get some old umbrellas and try it!
5. Kite propulsion, Get the kite out. Lay back and drift off. Good flying!
6. Use a group shelter or bivvy bag as a sail.
7. All the crew move back in the raft to raise the bows so they act as a sail. *Loel Collins*

Karl Midlane

CANOE GAMES

LOTS OF GEAR

Create your raft with as many boats as you want, secure with planks and gazspars to make assault courses to cross from boat to boat, balance beams, postman s walk, etc.

Loel Collins

www.outdooradventure.co.uk

SURF, SEA & BEACH GAMES ────────

SURF, SEA & BEACH GAMES

Game	Boat	Skill Development.	Level	Stroke	Good?
SURF					
330. Rugby tackle	KS	Edging, leaning, slipping, sliding, active posture, balance, bracing.	3-4	Support strokes	
331. Human wave	n/a	Visualising a run, planning, dodging.	4-5	Various	
332. Soup turns	KS	Active posture, turning, power transfer.	3-4	Turns.	
333. Beached seals	K	Launching, active posture, push/pull.	3-4	N/A	
334. Virtual wave	n/a	Visualising a run, planning, dodging.	4-5	Various	
335. Cardboard surf kayaks	n/a	Visualising a run, planning, dodging, Imagination and creative skills.	4-5	Various	
SEA					
340. Sea Monsters	KS	N/A	2-3	N/A	
341. Chart symbol snap	K	Symbol and shape recognition	3-5	N/A	
342. Build a bird	K	Bio-diversity, adaptation, observation.	1-5	N/A	
343. Mini beast bingo	K	Environmental awareness, bio-diversity.	1-4	N/A	
344. Write your name	K	Turns, co-ordination, imagination, visual awareness and control.	1-4	Various	
345. Life boats launch	K	Movement, sliding, balance, speed, posture.	2-3	Support strokes	
BEACH					
350. Blind fold feel	n/a	Biodiversity, environmental awareness	1-5	N/A	
351. Colour match	n/a	Biodiversity, environmental awareness	1-5	N/A	
352. Texture match	n/a	Biodiversity, environmental awareness	1-5	N/A	
353. Global Scavenge	n/a	Biodiversity, environmental awareness	1-5	N/A	
354. Beach fashion	n/a	Biodiversity, environmental awareness	1-5	N/A	
355. Dive in and get it	K	Orientation, biodiversity, environmental awareness, balance, water and darkness confidence.	3-5	Rolling,	
356. Time and Tide	n/a	Environmental awareness	1-5	N/A	
357. Glass bottom buckets	n/a	Environmental awareness, balance.	1-5	N/A	

DRY = Dry Land Game

DAMP = Afloat but should stay dry

WET = Some chance of splashing and accidental capsize

SWIM = High probability of a swim or similar

330 Rugby Tackle

Level 3-4   KS

Support Strokes

Paddle out just far enough so that you are amongst the small white water waves. Now turn your kayak sideways and get rugby tackled from the side by the next white water wave. The key is to think like a rugby player - be strong and balanced, don't lean towards the beach or towards the wave as in both cases you're at risk of being knocked over.

Get comfortable - being tackled from the side with your paddles stretched out in front of you ready for a low brace if required. When you're feeling more confident hold your paddles up over your head, then in just one hand and then with a partner throw them away.

Whilst in a strong balanced position, try holding the kayak at different angles allowing it to be deflected without it catching the beachward edge or forcing you to loose your balance.   *Simon Hammond*

331 Human Wave

Level 4-5

Get everyone in the group to line up on the beach and link arms. This line of people represents a wave. One person stands in front of the line holding their paddles - this person is the surfer. Now get the line to walk up the beach at a steady slow pace, as the wave gets near to the surfer they'll need to start paddling for the take off, as the wave hits they catch the wave and then can simulate their ride across the wave, dropping out in front of the wave for bottom turns and coming back up to the wave for top turns all the time progressing diagonally across the face.

This is a great wave simulation game that really unlocks the concept of surfing across the face and at the same time getting closer to the beach.

Simon Hammond

KS

Turns

332 Soup Turns

Level 3-4

Draw a grid in the sand with the end of your paddle and list everyones initials down one side. Send everyone out into the surf but limit how far out they go to the start of the broken, white water waves. As a paddler surfs towards the beach count how many 180¡ turns they make in the white water and tally this alongside their initials. You can tally each wave separately or you could just have one total tally for the game. The paddlers will start to feel how to get their kayaks turning quickly by using the natural power of the wave and their own body movement.

You could develop this game for a variety of moves and also have negative points for moves that are out of control. *Simon Hammond*

333 Beached Seals

Level 3-4   K

Draw two lines on the sand about 3 metres apart. Get everyone to line their kayaks up on the first line. On the command GO everyone in the race starts to move themselves and their kayaks to the second line, first to cross wins. The game could be developed with the paddlers in a Le mans style start behind their kayaks racing to get in, get their spray decks on and then shuffle to the finish.

The game s aim is to help paddlers discover the best way of seal launching their kayaks from a shallow sloping sandy beach. It also gives them a chance to practice the time consuming art of getting their amazingly tight fitting spray decks on before their kayaks are filled by an on-coming wave.

Simon Hammond

334 Virtual Wave

Level 4-5

Sand dunes form a virtual wave, draw the wave onto the dune so it shows the break and direction. People can stand with paddle in hands at the top of the dune and take off down the dune as if it s a wave, crank in a bottom turn and try a whole run, over the whole face of the dune as if it s a wave.

Loel Collins

335 Cardboard Surf Kayaks

Level 4-5

The evening before your session, give everyone some corrugated cardboard boxes and parcel tape and ask them to build a representation of a surf kayak to hang around their waist. Then try the Virtual Wave game above. It s a hoot.

CARDBOARD
& STICKY TAPE

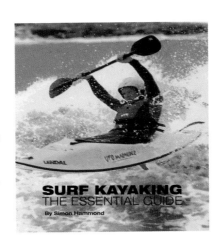

Surf Kayaking -

The Essential Guide

By Simon Hammond

World Surf Kayak Champion

ISBN 0-9550520-0-9

De-mystifies the art of surf kayaking .

Many games listed elsewhere in the book can be played on the sea, but here are a few special ones.

www.outdooradventure.co.uk

 KS

340 Sea Monsters

Level 2-3

Using the sea weed washed onto the beach the group have to make a sea monster ready for the paddle home. This could be one member from each team, or everyone dresses up as a sea monster.

 K

WATERPROOF CARDS

341 Chart Symbol Snap

Level 3-5

This game can be played in two ways;

1. Make a set of waterproof cards that have on them the symbols used on nautical charts, make a second set of cards with the definitions on. You put a definition down and whoever has the symbol shouts snap and throws the symbol on top and can pick up the cards, Whoever has most pairs wins

2. With the same cards, this time select from the pack those cards that represent symbols of buoys or other points on your trip. Hand these out and that person has to show you (and then perhaps take you) to that very point.

The same game can be played with map symbols.

Rosemary Powell

342 Build A Bird

Level 1-5 K

As you paddle with your group, point out the different birds on route. Make sure you talk about where the bird lives, what it eats and how it feeds. When you get to lunch get the group to look at the terrain close to where they ve landed. From what you can work out, what would a bird need to be like if it was to live and have lunch with us.

Muddy estuaries may need long beaks to get the worms from the mud, or long legs for when the tide comes in. On cliffy shorelines the birds who live low down might fish for food underwater so they need sharp beaks webbed feet and streamlined bodies. High up on the cliffs the birds will fly and dive, big wings, etc. I m sure you get the idea.

Loel Collins

343 Mini Beast Bingo

Level 1-4 K

WATERPROOF CARDS

Get one of those sea shore wildlife books, an old one, cut out the pictures and put them onto bingo cards, when you see one of the animals, birds or plants you can tick it off, when you ve seen them all you shout, Guhumphdemufdiguff! - It s an ancient cure for sea sickness.

Charlie Stretton

www.outdooradventure.co.uk

SURF, SEA & BEACH GAMES

K

344 Write Your Name

Level 1-4

On flat calm/glassy days try this game, which I use it to help sea kayaking skills. I ask the group to imagine that there is a person on the headland looking down on the group. Using the kayak as a big pen they have to write their name on the surface of the water - the wake of the boat should leave a trail that can be seen from above and obviously this has to be joined up writing. This is a great game for encouraging people to vary the radius of their turns and keep the boat moving.

Loel Collins

K

Support Strokes

345 Life Boats Launch

Level 2-3

On boulder beeches, move the smaller boulders to make a slide down the beech, Then you can launch your boats down the beech, best done with plastic boats, helmets and hands up. Yes of course this is a seal launch, but this can be much longer and more like an Alpine luge run!

Loel Collins

BEACH GAMES

Many of the other games in this book are great to play on the beach, but here are some special ones that take advantage of the marine environment and are ideal for after lunch, or whilst waiting for the tide to turn. Unfortunately beaches are not always the cleanest of environments so before any game it s a good idea to have a walk around and remove anything dangerous, unhealthy or risky. Consider marking out a playing area and brief your group not to touch anything they are unsure of. Remember Jelly fish can sting and sea urchins have spines!

www.outdooradventure.co.uk

350 Blind Fold Feel   Level 1-5

Pair your group up, one person in the pair is blindfolded and taken to a rock pool. In the rock pool their partner lets them feel something, let them have a good feel, then their blindfold is removed and they have to find and identify what ever it is they think they felt.

Loel Collins

351 Colour Match   Level 1-5

COLOUR TEST CARDS

Get some paint colour test cards from your local hardware store. The game is to find something natural on the beech that matches the colours on the cards. Blues greens, browns all work well. Find some similar cards with brighter colours and try to find unnatural things to match the colour.

Mark Walker

MATERIALS

352 Texture Match

Level 1-5

Take with you a selection of different materials that have a distinctive texture, let the group pass them around and then they have to find something on the beech that has similar texture, sand paper, glass, crumpled papers, chamois leather, wet leather, rubber, etc...

Charlotte Stretton

RUBBER GLOVES
& SACKS

353 Global Scavenge

Level 1-5

On some beaches you can collect loads of rubbish so why not think about playing a game to help clear the beach? For example:
Before we go every one has to find 5 bits of rubbish to take home.
Lets see how many different countries we can find rubbish from.
Lets sea how old the rubbish can be?

Loel Collins

354 Beach Fashion

Level 1-5

Divide the group into teams and from what they can find on the beach each team has to design this years fashion clothes and arrange a modelling parade.

Loel Collins

355 Dive In & Get It
Level 3-5

SWIM GOGGLES
Rolling

This can be a team or individual game; for some it can be just a really good visual experience. Ask players to bring along an old pair of goggles. Players just put the goggles on and turn over in their kayaks. If they cannot roll then divide the group into pairs so that they can help each other. This can be done in lakes, or best of all in the sea along the rocky coast, especially if the water is very clear and there is a shipwreck in the shallows. If you do it at night, using a torch helps; the frequently-seen little red dots are crabs' eyes. Make sure torches are water-proof. You can turn the exercise into a game when you are in shallow waters by shouting out objects players have to find; tell them to reach down and bring to the surface things like stones, weeds or fish.

356 Time & Tide
Level 1-5

If at any time you find yourself pausing next to the sea, take the opportunity to mark the waters edge. Come back a little later and a noticeable change in height can be observed in just a few minutes. This is an ideal thing to do whilst adjusting foot rests at the start of a trip or during a lunch stop.

For best results choose the section of shoreline with the gentlest of gradients as you will find that this will exaggerate the change. If the tide is ebbing then a simple line drawn in the sand or mud will suffice, and after just a few minutes the water will no longer come up to your line. A flooding tide will soon cover your mark so something more substantial will be needed; a small pile of rocks or paddle stuck in the sand is ideal. If you are unsure yourself what the tide is doing then the flooding option will cover all eventualities. Whatever you choose, get your students involved as much as possible.

The success of this exercise will depend on your tidal range, so on the west coast of Ireland you will get a significant change in just five minutes, but if you work on the Mediterranean it is probably not worth bothering with. Fresh water coaches may still find this worthwhile, monitoring the water level in your local lake can give interesting variations over a period of several weeks and if you are operating in a river environment the unpredictable levels of rivers can be monitored over lunch.

357 Glass Bottom Buckets
Level 1-5

CLING FILM
& PLASTIC POTS

A bucket with its bottom cut out and replaced with a sheet of glass or clear plastic can give a good view of the life below the water when the glass end is pressed just below the surface, but not deep enough to flood the bucket. This works like a diving mask but does not need strapping to the face. The glass can easily be scratched and become useless so consider cheaper, disposable home made options that may be as low key as a bit of cling film taped over the end of a bottomless yoghurt pot. Be warned though, trying to peer into the bucket whilst still in your boat often leads to capsizes. *Karl Midlane*

WHITE WATER GAMES

White water training and practice can often get very serious, and one or two games are a great help at getting people to loosen up and to use their river running skills without thinking too deeply.

Great care obviously needs to be taken to select the right rapids and the right games for your paddlers. Players should be happy, confident, and be familiar with the white water they are playing on - for example the games you see illustrated here were all photographed at the Welsh National White Water Centre on the Afon Tryweryn, a class 3+ river, however the players were all grade 4+ paddlers and very familiar with the river.

Game	Boat	Skill Development.	Level	Stroke	Good?
360 Follow the leader	CK	All WW skills, observing skills, vision, dynamic posture, control, speed, edge, angle, trim.	4-5	All	
361 Change your class	CK	As above.	4-5	All	
362 How many times can you stop	CK	Observation, control, speed, vision, analysis.	4-5	Breaking in and out.	
363 Run Away	CK	Prediction, reaction, vision, problem solving.	4-5	All	
364 Only reverse strokes	CK	Feel for water, time awareness.	4-5	Reverse strokes, reverse ferry.	
365 Sideways only	K	Rotation, active posture, balance, vision, angle, edge, push/pull, dodging, timing	5	Forward, reverse	
366 Stern first	CK	As above	4-5	All	
367 Last one down wins	CK	Control, speed, group awareness.	4-5	Breaking in and out.	
368 Eddy Chess	CK	All WW skills, observing skills, vision, dynamic posture, control, speed, edge, angle, trim.	4-5	All	
369 Waltzing	CK	Reading of water, control, turning.	4-5	Forward, reverse, breaking in and out.	
370 Snatch the hat	CK	All WW skills, observing skills, vision, dynamic posture, control, speed, edge, angle, trim, timing	4-5	All	
371 Snakes and ladders	CK	Identification of line, problem solving, reaction.	4-5	All	
372 Planes & gliders	CK	All WW skills, observing skills, vision, dynamic posture, control, speed, edge, angle, trim	4-5	All	
373 Drift Ball	CK	All WW skills, observing skills, vision, dynamic posture, control, speed, edge, angle, trim, timing	4-5	All	
374 Eddy line games	CK	Understanding of eddy of lines, rotation, reaction, co-operation, speed, control, feel	4	Sweep strokes.	
375 Eddy line tag	CK	As above	4-5	All	
376 Extreme follow the leader	CK	Reaction, All WW skills, observing skills, vision, dynamic posture, control, speed, edge, angle, trim, timing	5	All	
377 Line of sight	CK	Use of water, observation, analysis, group awareness.	5	All	
378 Pick an eddy	CK	Use of water, observation, analysis, group awareness.	5	All	
379 Eddy Golf	CK	Identification of line, use of water.	4-5	Breaking in and out.	

PLAYBOAT GAMES

Game	Boat	Skill Development.	Level	Stroke	Good?
390 Bow Stall on a partner	K	Control, balance, trim, reaction, feel	5	Bow stalls	
391 Bow rotations	K	Control, balance, trim, reaction, timing, rotation, co-operation.	5	Trim and slicing.	
392 Dry land balancing	CK	Control, balance, lean, edge, trim, reaction.	4-5	Balance and support	
393 Dry land rolling	K	Control, balance, lean, reaction, rotation.	1-5	Rolling	
394 Mogul turns	CK	Control, balance, lean, edge, trim, timing, rotation.	4-5	Sweep strokes, spins.	
395 Zig Zags.1	K	As above	4-5	Surfing	
396 Zig zags.2	K	Control, balance, lean, edge, trim, timing, rotation.	4-5	Surfing	

360 Follow the leader in rapids

Level 4-5   CK

This is like the normal game of follow-the-leader or team slalom. Besides the usual breaking in and out of eddies it can also involve lots of other moves such as sitting in stoppers, surfing waves, 360s, rock splats, cart wheels, etc. It can start easy, and then be made harder on subsequent runs. Follow a buddy on a wave for a freestyle run is similar and always fun.

Rob White

361 Change your class

Level 4-5   CK

The next time you are planning a white water trip, plan to take along a variety of different types of boats so that paddlers can swap around. Too many people stick to one class of canoe or kayak and never try the others - let alone on a small rapid. They could try anything from a play boat to a Down River Racing C2. This can be great fun.

362 How many times can you stop

Level 4-5   CK

Breaking in and out

Between a defined start and end count how many times you can stop. Use Eddies, Micro eddies, Seams, Waves, Holes, and with caution the upstream side of rocks.   *Dave Luke*

363 Run Away

Level 4-5   CK

BALL

Each paddler gets a beach ball or similar. As they approach the rapid they throw the ball in front of them (3-4 boat lengths). The paddler then has to follow the ball down the rapid without getting too close or losing it. They collect it at the bottom.   *Loel Collins*

CK

Reverse strokes,
reverse ferries.

364 Only reverse strokes
Level 4-5

Try running rapids only using reverse strokes. Being able to slow down is a primary skill, it buys you time to avoid hazards and plan your next move. As you reverse paddle down the river try visiting each bank a number of specified times. Check and set into eddies like an open canoeist.

Dave Luke

K

Forward, reverse

365 Sideways only
Level 5

It s so easy descending a river - the water s going downstream anyway, so why paddle that way? Place your boat sideways to the current and paddle forwards or backwards to line up with the route you have chosen.

Dave Luke

CK

366 Stern first
Level 4-5

If you happen to end up going down a rapid backwards by accident - it won t be too much of a surprise if you have practised beforehand

Dave Luke

CK

Breaking in and out

367 Last one down wins
Level 4-5

A competitive game based on the leapfrog leadership style. As soon as you find yourself at the front break out of the current into an eddy, when passed by the last person then you break back in. Rules are that you must stay close and your body must be down stream of the previous paddler.

Dave Luke

Rob White

CK

368 Eddy chess
Level 4-5

Pair your paddlers up of roughly equal ability. The first one enters the rapid and catches an eddy. As the second person enters the rapid the first indicates another eddy the person has to catch - making it either tricky or easy, but it should be possible. The second person catches (or tries to catch) the indicated eddy and then selects the next eddy for the first paddler to try and catch. This is repeated to the bottom of the rapid.

Loel Collins

369 Waltzing
Level 4-5 CK

Forward, reverse, breaking in and out

Find a stretch of river with loads of good eddies. Paddle gently toward the first eddy (as if your breaking out) BUT as the bow of the boat crosses the eddy line, use a strong reverse sweep to spin the boat without fully breaking out. Now paddle backwards towards the next eddy, as the back starts to enter the eddy use a forwards sweep to spin the boat to face downstream again without entering the eddy. Now go forwards towards the next eddy and repeat the process down the whole rapid picking eddies going forwards and backwards round and round.

Marcus Bailie

370 Snatch the hat
Level 4-5 CK

HAT

This game is played on playful rapids. One person wears a hat on top of their safety helmet. Once the hat is on their head they are not allowed to touch it. The other players have to try and grab the hat and put it on their own head. Take care that players are not too vigorous when playing this game.

Rob White

371 Snakes and ladders
Level 4-5 CK

Pick your rapid carefully! Sit at the top or inspect and get your group to decide how far down the rapid they can go and still get back to the top using eddies, waves and water features.
Alternatively, run the rapid with your group getting them to move around the rapid picking features and routes to try and get back up. When you get to the bottom let them try to get back up. *Loel Collins*

372 Planes and gliders
Level 4-5 CK

The eddies in the rapid are landing strips for air planes. On their first run the group have to land their airplanes (their boats) in is many eddies as possible. They then repeat the run but this time they only have gliders so are not allowed to use power and have to use a minimum of paddling - they have to use the water currents, waves etc to get to each eddy/landing strip.

Loel Collins

BALL

373 Drift Ball (Driftwood)

Level 4-5

This is a game for moving water in which you can teach paddlers how to move quickly, and so build confidence. Line up the paddlers along the bank in their boats ready to paddle. Throw a ball upstream and shout out instructions to the paddlers such as. 'Paddle to the middle of the river'. 'Go around the ball as it is floating down the river', 'Go around the ball twice'.

All this has to be completed before the ball reaches a certain marker such as a bridge. This can either be done individually or as a group. You can make it as hard and involved as you think the group can manage. If you have no ball then a piece of driftwood can be used instead.

Rob White

374 Eddy line games

Level 4

Sweep strokes

Find a good eddy line. How many spins can you do with as few a strokes as possible? Try going with it or against it, both ways, How about eyes shut?, How about without a paddle stroke, or without removing the paddle from the water?

Loel Collins

375 Eddy line tag

Level 4-5

The first paddler goes downstream, finds an eddy, goes into it facing upstream and holds their hand out a foot or so above the water. The second paddler has to get to the same eddy and slap the first paddlers hand, then set straight off to find the next eddy, hold their hand out and see if the first paddler can get to their eddy, and so on. This works as a challenge trying to find hard or small eddies and pushes the second paddler to follow and hit the same eddy. It is a great exercise to warm groups up on long winter paddling days.

Andrew Craven

376 Extreme follow the leader

Level 5

If you cant touch the boat in front you are too far behind. Exciting and for good paddlers only!

Dave Luke

Rob White

377 Line of sight
Level 5   CK

Allow your group to enter a rapid, each boat has to take an eddy so they can see the rest of the group. Once all are in place, the upstream paddler has to paddle past the group to the next eddy where they can see the whole group. This moves you on and downstream as far as you want.

Pete Catteral

378 Pick an eddy
Level 5   CK

Use this game only when you can see the whole rapid - it works well in rapids with large boulders. Collect your group at the top of a rapid. The idea is to allow your group into the rapid (one at a time). Each member of the group has to pick an eddy so they can see other members of the group. As they leave the first eddy you have to tell them how many other team members they have to be able to see from the final eddy they choose.

John Spike Green

379 Eddy Golf
Level 4-5   CK

Breaking in and out

Two teams line up on opposite sides of a rectangular playing area. One team have plastic ducks (or other suitable buoyant objects) sitting on their front decks. They have to make their way from one side of the area to the other running a gauntlet as the opposition try to dislodge the ducks by splashing as they pass. The number of ducks still in position on completing the crossing indicates the points scored. The opposition then take their turn.

Rob White

K

Bow stalls

390 Bow Stall on a partner
Level 5

One paddler bow stalls their boat off the side of fellow paddler's boat and then tries to move their boat all the way around the other boat and back to the starting point without falling over.   *Caroline Gerritsen*

Peter Knowles

 K

Trim and Slicing

391 Bow rotations
Level 5

Two paddlers face each other. Number one slices her bow under and the other lifts his bow over the other boat. Keep rotating around each other for as long as possible. Start off as a pair but once you are accomplished you can add other paddlers to form a line so the new paddler rotates their bow around the stern of one of the paddlers of the original two. The aim is of course to get as many people involved as possible.

Caroline Gerritsen

392 Dry land balancing

Level 4-5 CK

Balance your boat on edge for as long as possible. Initially allow pushing off the floor and stabilising with hands but work up to a completely clean move. *Caroline Gerritsen*

Balance and support

Peter Knowles

393 Dry land rolling

Level 1-5 K

Make sure the boats aren't too heavy! Sit in the boat, roll over on edge (with your back on the grass), then pull the boat over on top, set up and sweep or C to C roll as you wish. *Caroline Gerritsen*

Rolling

394 Mogul turns

Level 4-5 CK

Find a wave train, float down onto it - your object is to see how many times you can flat spin the boat in the wave train, only turning on the tops of the waves. Or, as a variation, try only turning in the troughs.

Loel Collins

Sweep strokes, spins

395 Zig Zags 1.

Level 4-5 K

On the same wave train, try turning the boat to the left on the top of the first wave, to the right on the second, left on the third etc. *Loel Collins*

Sweep strokes

396 Zig zags.2

Level 4-5 K

Start from an eddy surf diagonally across the face of the first wave, surf back across the second, back across on the third etc. — all the way down the wave train. *Loel Collins*

Surfing

The younger generation, in their flat boats, looked on in awe as Eric went airborne - "radical" they thought, "Is this the way that playboats will go?"

Appendix A List of Games

We all like making lists - here s a start, but please add your own!

Inclusive games

Most   Warm up games.
Most   Raft games
46   Bingo
48   Aqua Kayaking
49   Cowboys and Indians
51   Duck Races
52   Prui
60   Catch
61   Keep that ball up.
71   Fitness Ball Polo
72   Pass the Ball Polo
73   Blindfold Polo
82   Team Tag
96   Blindfold Rattler
98   Dragons Den
115   What s the time Mrs Wolf
119   Kayak Bridge
121   Evolution
156   Throwline surf
157   Animal Farm
224   Chariots
229   Macaroons
261   Jungle Chain Walk in
263   Amazon River journey
331   Human Wave
345   Life Boat launch

Quiet games

96   Blindfold Rattler
264   Duck Hunting
273   Who is teaching who?
274   Orienteering
335   Cardboard surf kayaks
351   Colour match
352   Texture match

K1 - Games for long thin boats

118   Synchronised paddling
119   Kayak bridge
127   Move to that spot
245   Bertie the tug boat
262   Follow my leader
270   Hold that spot
344   Write your name

Blindfold games

52   Prui
73   Blindfold Polo
96   Blindfold Rattler
113   Listen to the Leader
123   Paparazzi
144   Guide Dogs
158   Night Time Animals
340   Blindfold beach feel

Horrid aggressive games

45   Hacky Thump
49   Cowboys and Indians
50   Dolphins
63   Polo
88   Sharks and Dolphins
141   Greasy Pole
154   Jousting
275   Hunt the keys
321   Walking the plank

Long Term Paddler Development

In 2004 the BCU started work to develop a Long Term Paddler Development (LTPD) model to suit paddlesport, based on the work of Dr Istvan Balyi on Long term Athlete Development. This athlete development strategy has been established based on the principles behind human growth and development and maximises the opportunities this offers to the paddler. The model aims to provide a base of paddlesport and movement skills that will give an individual the opportunity to enjoy our sport to whatever level they choose, whether recreationally or high performance. It also aims to help deliverers provide the right opportunities at the right time, ensuring that paddlers are enjoying paddlesport and progressing at an optimal level.

The Long Term Paddler Develop ment model supports paddlers from the day they first get into a boat over a span of many years, providing a logical progression of programme planning and skill development from the young paddler to the experienced performer.

At each stage specific principles and guidelines for physical, psychological, technical, tactical and ancillary development are identified.

Once competencies have been achieved at one level, they form the foundation for the next level. The model takes the paddler from basic to complex skills, from general to specific, and from beginner to expert. It considers what the paddler should be doing and when, providing the best possible programme to ensure individuals come into the sport, stay in the sport and achieve performances that reflect their potential / aspirations.

The first phase of the model (the Foundation paddlesport phase) focuses on developing quality skills through enjoyable and appropriate activities, giving paddlers skills to allow them to progress either down a recreational or performance route depending upon their aspirations.

This Canoe Games book provides a huge resource of games and activities that can be used to promote the skill development that is so crucial in the first few years of a paddler s career. However, simply by playing the games does not automatically create skilful paddlers. Games provide a fantastic opportunity for the coach to develop quality movements in a fun and positive learning environment. The skill of coaching is to select appropriate games and have a clear idea about how you can use them to develop certain skills.

DISCOVER THE BEST OF BRITAIN'S PADDLES

AN ESSENTIAL MAP FOR ANYONE WHO LOVES TO EXPLORE IN A KAYAK, CANOE OR SIT ON TOP

SCALE 1:625,000

CANOE & KAYAK MAP OF BRITAIN

RIVERS PUBLISHING

Great value at £9.95
UK National Best Seller

"A kayak and canoeist dream pin up!

A great wall map of Britain's water ways, both sides of map, with website links and info of the area's canoe sites and shops, canoe trails, guide books and info on rules and regulations with further links! Brilliant buy for all levels. 5 stars!"

Independent review on Amazon

INDEX

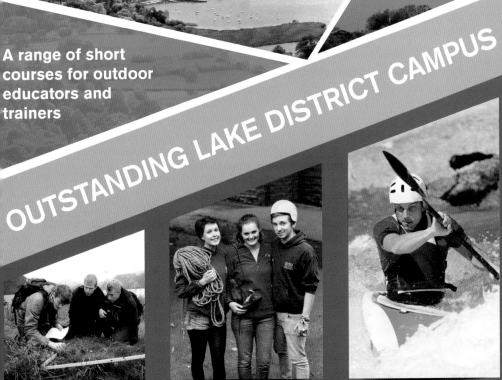

Get qualified for the
OUTDOORS

Undergraduate and Postgraduate courses in outdoor leadership, education and environment

A range of short courses for outdoor educators and trainers

OUTSTANDING LAKE DISTRICT CAMPUS

Find out more: www.cumbria.ac.uk/outdoors

 enquirycentre@cumbria.ac.uk

0845 606 1144

University of **Cumbria**

Keswick Climbing Wall & Newlands Adventure Centre

Indoor & Outdoor Adventures For All Ages.

- Indoor Climbing
- Indoor & Outdoor Archery
- Ghyll Scramble
- 170m Zip Wire
- Canoeing
- High Ropes

- Rookery Woods Adventure Play
- Outdoor Rock Climb
- Kayaking
- Orienteering
- Indoor Bouldering
- Hill Walking

FREE ALL DAY PARKING

KESWICK CLIMBING WALL

Goosewell Farm, Keswick,
Cumbria, CA12 4RN

TEL: 017687 72000

www.keswickclimbingwall.co.uk

NEWLANDS ADVENTURE CENTRE

Stair, Keswick,
Cumbria, CA12 5UF

TEL: 017687 78463

www.activity-centre.com

Jackson Kayak

sportscotland
glenmorelodge
national **outdoor** training centre

hōu canoes

PE▲KUK
www.peakuk.com

WERNER
PADDLES

Inspiring
Adventure

www.glenmorelodge.org.uk

We are Scotland's National Outdoor Training Centre located in the heart of Cairngorms National Park. Learn, develop or qualify in an adventure sport of your choice. Our goal is to inspire adventure by teaching beginners, coaching intermediate/advanced and delivering training and assessment courses for leaders and instructors.

Photo: Ed Smith

White water | Open canoeing | Sea kayaking | Surf kayaking | First aid and rescue & Qualifications

QUALITY PADDLESPORT COACHING & COURSES

Don't play around with your kit, get all the best deals

DESPERATE MEASURES

We have it all from centre kayaks and the latest white water boats, to safety equipment and practical accessories. You will find our fresh informative and knowledgeable staff will guide you through any purchase - over the phone, online, or at our extensive show rooms. Instructors - remember to ask about our centre staff scheme.

www.desperate-measures.co.uk
telephone 0115 981 6815
39-41 Trent Boulevard,
West Bridgford,
Nottingham NG2 5BB

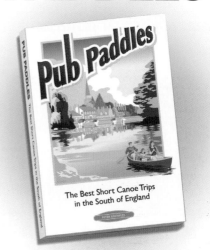

FUN STUFF

gear for paddlers

palmequipmenteurope.com